EASY HOME COOKING

Easy Home Cooking

Classic Recipes That Prep in 15 Minutes

Linda Larsen

Photography by Marija Vidal

ROCKRIDGE PRESS

For general information on our other products and services or to obtain technical support, please contact our Customer Care Department within the United States at (866) 744-2665, or outside the United States at (510) 253-0500.

Rockridge Press publishes its books in a variety of electronic and print formats. Some content that appears in print may not be available in electronic books, and vice versa.

TRADEMARKS: Rockridge Press and the Rockridge Press logo are trademarks or registered trademarks of Callisto Media Inc. and/or its affiliates, in the United States and other countries, and may not be used without written permission. All other trademarks are the property of their respective owners. Rockridge Press is not associated with any product or vendor mentioned in this book.

Interior and Cover Designer: Scott Petrower
Art Producer: Karen Williams
Editor: Adrian Potts
Production Editor: Rachel Taenzler

Photography © 2020 Marija Vidal. Food styled by Elisabet der Nederlanden.
Author photo © 2020 Picture This Photography Portrait Studio.
Cover: Chicken Cacciatore, page 76

ISBN: Print 978-1-64739-866-8 | eBook 978-1-64739-544-5
R0

To my wonderful family: my husband Doug,
my parents Duane and Marlene, my sisters Laura and Lisa,
and my nieces and nephew Maddie, Grace, and Michael.
They have been so supportive of my career, and happily eaten
anything I have cooked, even since I was 10 years old.

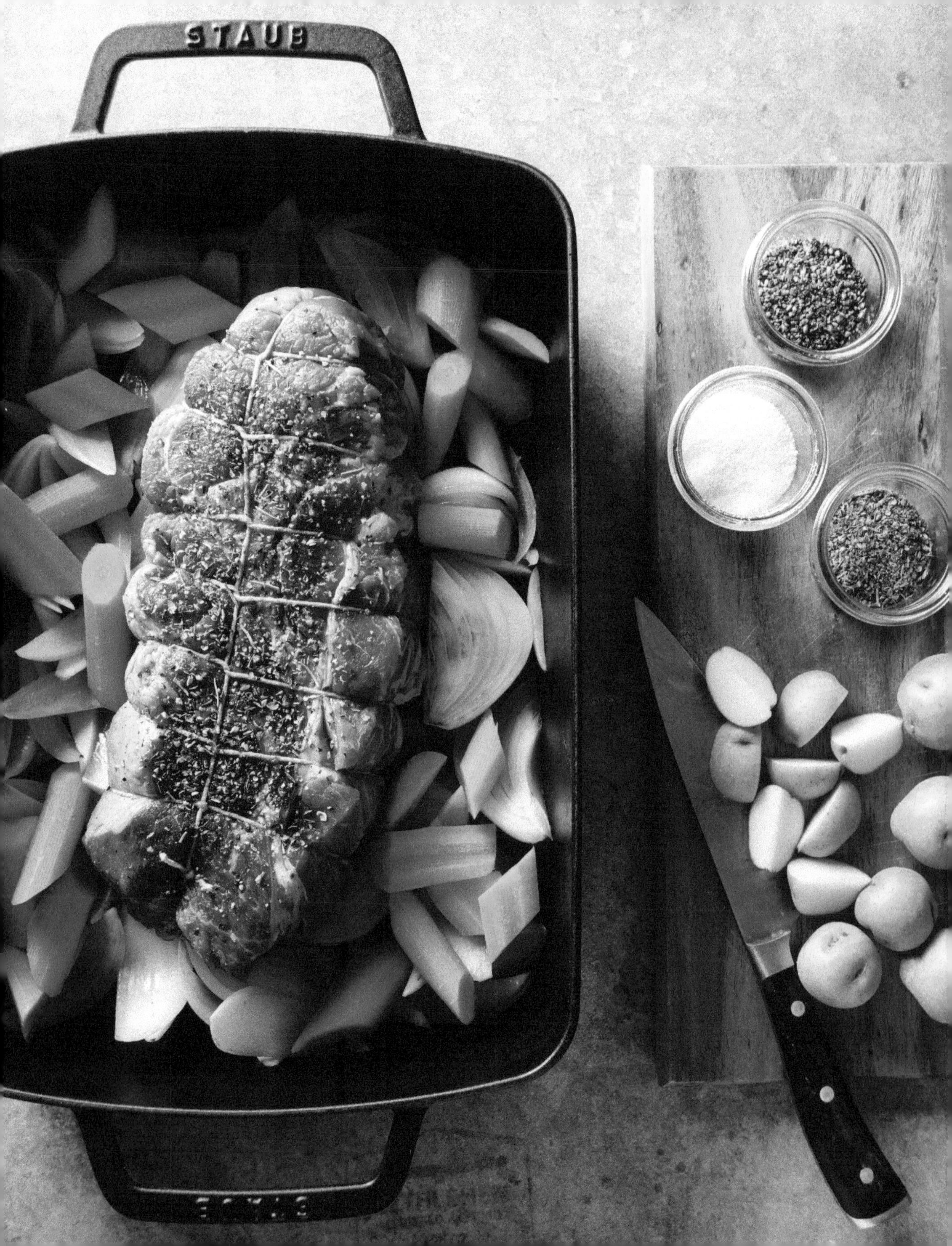
STAUB

Contents

Introduction

Home cooking is the best kind of cooking: classic dishes that are comforting and delicious but easy to make. This is my 45th cookbook and is probably my favorite. I began in the kitchen cooking from classic cookbooks such as Fanny Farmer, Better Homes & Gardens, Pillsbury, the *Joy of Cooking*, and Betty Crocker. Most of these books were my mother's and grandmothers', written in the 1940s, 1950s, and 1960s, a time that I think represents American cooking at its best. Women and men knew how to cook then. From scratch. And everyone ate three square meals a day, all served around the kitchen or dining room table.

I made bread from scratch, all kinds of layer cakes, homey casseroles, lots of scalloped potatoes, crackers, salads, and meat and poultry dishes. I learned to cook from these cookbooks and would read them as if they were fiction. In fact, I often sneaked peeks at books during family meals! That was definitely frowned upon, but I persisted.

As my cooking interest expanded, I did dive into international cuisines, most notably French (thanks to Julia Child) and Tex-Mex (because of trips to the Southwest my family took when I was young). I actually did make puff pastry from scratch (and haven't attempted it since), and my biggest triumph was French pastries made from one of Julia's books. But I still return to American home cooking when I want to make something reliable, easy, and comforting.

One of my degrees is in Food Science and Nutrition. I actually did work for Pillsbury on the Pillsbury Bake-Off for years, which was a lifelong dream. From there, I started writing online and learned how wonderful it was to teach people how to cook and help solve problems. My biggest interest is helping beginning cooks navigate their way around the kitchen and showing them that cooking and baking are skills that anyone can learn, given a bit of effort and ambition. That's the focus of this book.

But this book is also going to help people who are confident in the kitchen and want to expand their recipe repertoires and get ideas for putting their own spins on the food they cook and bake. These recipes are simple enough to entice beginners, but interesting enough to appeal to those with more kitchen skills. Among the recipes, you'll find comfort classics prepared with a special twist, along with contemporary dishes that have creative flavor combinations.

So, join me as we navigate kitchen adventures. You'll learn how to prep ingredients quickly and efficiently, learn how to make the most of fresh foods, learn some valuable kitchen tips, and enjoy serving these recipes to family and friends. I promise you'll have a lot of fun.

CHAPTER ONE

Easy Home Cooking

Did you know that you can get bread into the oven in 15 minutes, and prep a pot roast in that same amount of time? Even if you love to cook and putter around the kitchen, everyone needs recipes that don't take a lot of hands-on time but still produce wonderful results. Some days you may want to make a three-layer cake or an elaborate main-dish salad, but many times you want to get in and out of the kitchen as quickly as possible. That's where this book comes to the rescue.

You'll learn about mise en place, how to measure more quickly, and some shortcuts using ingredients you probably didn't know about. You will be working at a pretty fast clip, but all these recipes are simple and easy enough to prepare that 15 minutes is doable. Then you can relax while the food chills, or simmers, or bakes in the oven.

The Joy of Home Cooking

So, what is home cooking? It is, quite simply, food cooked at home, food that is uncomplicated, delicious, and easy to make. Home cooking recipes include meatloaf, a roast chicken, a basic pie or cake, casseroles, and fresh salads. Although most everyone loves eating out at restaurants and enjoys the occasional fast-food meal, those aren't the foods that feed your soul.

Home cooking is inspired by the kind of food our grandmothers made. These recipes are classic, comforting, and suited to modern tastes, without being fussy or calling for unusual ingredients. There's something inherently satisfying about being able to create dishes that will feed and nourish your family. These recipes use inexpensive ingredients and don't take a lot of effort. There is a time and place for making a meal that requires 20 steps and 30 ingredients, but that isn't true of home cooking.

The demands of modern living put pressure on us all. Even if you have all the appliances on the market in your home, with the demands of work, parenting, and commuting, it seems there is less and less time to enjoy a home-cooked meal around the dinner table. All too often, it seems so much easier to pick up some takeout on the way home, use a food delivery service, or heat up a processed and packaged meal from the freezer.

But as the recipes in this book will prove, enjoying simple home cooking is not only more satisfying, it will save you money and your diet will be healthier. I once worked briefly in a restaurant kitchen and was appalled when I saw how line cooks upended salt containers into soup and the amount of fat they used in each recipe.

Your diet and life will improve immeasurably by the simple act of cooking at home. Not only are you keeping alive a valuable tradition, you may even be teaching your kids a lifelong skill.

15 Minutes Hands-On Time

All the recipes in this book have been designed for just 15 minutes of hands-on prep time before the food goes onto the stove, into the oven, or right onto the dinner table. The recipes include speedy-to-serve salads and sides, quick-cooking main dishes, and some fast-to-fix comfort foods that can bake or simmer for hours while you do other things around the house.

Although the average home cook should be able to wash, cut, chop, and prepare these recipes in 15 minutes or less, just how quickly you can achieve these tasks will likely depend on your experience in the kitchen. After all, if you've never chopped an onion before, it will take you more time to accomplish that task than it would someone who has been chopping and prepping vegetables for years. But take heart: As you gain experience in the kitchen, your skills will improve, and prep time will decrease. And remember that it's far safer to take your time and work deliberately if you are new to the kitchen. Stopping to bandage a knife injury will slow you down more than being careful in the first place.

The quick preparation time will also make the dreaded kitchen task of cleanup faster and easier. You won't have to deal with a sink full of utensils, mixing bowls, pots, and pans with these recipes. Many use just one bowl, pan, or skillet, along with a few measuring cups and utensils.

5 WAYS TO SPEED UP PREP

There are some specific things you can do that will automatically speed up food preparation time. As you integrate these practices into your everyday cooking, you'll find that you won't even have to think about them anymore.

1. **Get a sharp chef's knife and learn how to use it.** Look online for well-rated knives or go to a specialty store and ask for advice. And study some of the many online tutorials about the proper way to hold and use a knife.

2. **Prep food as you unpack it from the store.** One of the best ways to get a jump on food preparation is to do some minimal prepping as you unpack groceries—be it by browning some ground beef that you'll use in tomorrow's chili and refrigerating it, or washing and slicing produce such as celery and bell peppers.

3. **Buy strips of meat or frozen veggies.** Stores often sell meat already sliced for dishes like stir-fries. Plain frozen veggies typically retain all the nutrients of fresh foods and can make a big difference in prep time.

4. **Mise en place.** This French concept simply means to gather all the ingredients and equipment you'll need for a recipe before you start. This way, you don't need to stop in the middle of prep to search for a spice or a whisk.

5. **Plan ahead.** Making a plan for the recipes you'll cook for a few days or a week will save lots of time. Shop for those foods and then make the recipes. You won't have to spend any time thinking about what's for dinner, and you know you will have all the ingredients you need.

The Home Kitchen

One of the best things about home cooking is that you'll need only basic kitchen equipment to make the meals in this book. There's no need to buy a food processor, cutlet bat, pressure cooker, or a huge, expensive stand mixer.

Equipment and Tools

The Basics

These are the essential tools and equipment you'll need for the recipes.

Baking dishes: These can be ceramic, metal, or glass as long as they are ovenproof. The recipes mostly call for a 9-by-13-inch (3-quart) baking dish, and some a 9-inch square (2½-quart) baking dish. You'll also need a 9-by-5-inch loaf pan for making bread.

Baking sheet: This is used both as a baking sheet and to make one-pan dinners. Get one rimmed baking sheet and one without sides.

Basic utensils: A grater, vegetable peeler, and whisk are needed for these recipes. A grater lets you shred cheese in seconds. And a whisk will remove lumps from sauces in no time.

Spatulas: Silicone spatulas, which are heatproof, let you get every drop of batter out of a bowl as well as stir ingredients in a pan. And thin and flat metal spatulas are essential for transferring food from a pan to a cooling rack.

Hot pads or oven mitts: To safely remove hot pans from the oven, pads or mitts are essential. Get several because they will get dirty when you're handling food.

Knife set: Although you don't need to spend a fortune, it pays to buy the best you can afford. Get a set with a chef's knife and a few paring knives.

Measuring cups and spoons: Get a set of metal measuring cups for dry ingredients, a set of measuring spoons, and a glass measuring cup for liquids.

Nonstick skillet: This type of skillet is best for sautéing and browning foods. The newest types will not flake or degrade.

Saucepan, stockpot, and skillet: A good set of pots and pans will last a lifetime. A saucepan is deeper than a skillet, 6 to 8 inches deep, and has a smaller diameter. A skillet is used to shallow-fry food and has a larger diameter than a saucepan; they are usually about 2 to 3 inches deep. A stockpot is wide and 10 to 14 inches deep, used to hold quarts of soups and stocks as they simmer and to cook pasta.

Nice-to-Haves

These items are not necessary for most of the recipes, but are suggested from time to time.

Baking basics: Some recipes for baked goods call for a wire rack, a 12-cup muffin tin, or a 9-inch springform pan (which has sides that release with a hinge to serve).

Blender: Although not a necessity, this is nice to have if you want to quickly blend together ingredients, soups, or sauces.

Broiler pan: Most ovens come with broiler pans, which consist of a slotted pan on top of another shallow pan to catch drippings.

Dutch oven: This large pot with a lid can cook food on the stove or in the oven.

Parfait glasses: These come in handy for the Apple Yogurt Parfait (page 13) and Chocolate Eton Mess (page 117), though you can improvise with other types of glasses or mason jars.

Wok: A wok is a nice, but not necessary, pan to have for dishes like fried rice and stir-fries, though a large skillet will work just as well.

SAFELY COOKING MEAT, SHELLFISH, AND EGGS

A food thermometer is an indispensable item for the home cook. Not only will it tell you when certain foods are at their most tender so you don't overcook them, but more importantly, it will tell you when they are safe to eat. This is most necessary for ground beef, pork, shellfish, eggs, and whole cuts of chicken and turkey, which can contain bacteria that can make you sick.

You can find thermometers at all price ranges on Amazon, in grocery stores, and in cooking equipment stores. Buy the best you can afford.

Although the recipes in this book include cues that can help you guess at doneness, the only way to be sure is to use a thermometer, especially if you are cooking for someone very young, elderly, pregnant, or who has a chronic illness, who may have serious complications from a foodborne illness. Easy-to-follow thermometer guidance is provided as required throughout the book to make mealtime as safe as possible.

Making the Recipes

The exact preparation time is included in each recipe along with the cook time. Cooking time is usually fast unless it's a dish like a pot roast that will cook away happily while you do other things. These labels on every recipe will help you decide which ones you want to make, depending on your food preferences and/or allergies.

One Pan/One Pot
Only requires one pot or pan.

Under 30 Minutes
These recipes can be prepped, cooked, and served in 30 minutes or less.

5-Ingredient
Recipes with this label only use five ingredients (not counting salt, pepper, or oil).

Freezer Friendly
These recipes can be frozen for later use and will reheat beautifully.

Dairy-Free
These recipes do not use any dairy ingredients such as butter, milk, cream, sour cream, or cheese.

Gluten-Free
These recipes do not contain any ingredients with gluten, including wheat flours, wheat bran, cracked wheat, farro, barley, wheat pasta, or semolina.

Classic Blueberry
Pancakes, page 21

CHAPTER TWO
Breakfasts and Brunches

Oatmeal Jam Muffins

Prep time: 15 minutes   **Cook time:** 15 minutes   **Makes 12 muffins**

Muffins are often one of the first recipes that beginning cooks learn to make. That doesn't mean they have to be boring or uninspiring. These muffins are made with oatmeal for tenderness and texture and have a surprise jam center that adds great flavor and interest. They are perfect for breakfast on the run.

Nonstick baking spray

1½ cups all-purpose flour

½ cup quick-cooking oats

½ cup packed light brown sugar

1 teaspoon baking powder

Pinch salt

2 large eggs

½ cup whole milk

⅓ cup jam, any flavor

1. Preheat the oven to 350°F. Coat a 12-cup muffin tin with baking spray or line with paper liners and set aside.

2. In a large bowl, combine the flour, oats, brown sugar, baking powder, and salt and mix well.

3. In a glass measuring cup or a bowl, beat the eggs and milk until combined.

4. Add the egg mixture to the flour mixture and stir just until combined. Do not overmix or the muffins will be tough. Some lumps are fine.

5. Divide the batter among the prepared muffin cups, filling each about three-quarters full. Put about 1 teaspoon of the jam on each muffin. Using the tip of a knife, swirl the jam into the muffin batter.

6. Bake the muffins for 15 to 20 minutes, until they are golden brown and firm to the touch. Remove from the muffin tin to cool on a wire rack for 30 minutes before serving.

Ingredient tip: Nonstick baking spray is a type of cooking spray that contains flour and is commonly used to keep baked goods like muffins, cakes, and cupcakes from sticking to the pan. Look for it in the baking section of the grocery store near the other nonstick cooking sprays.

Cooking tip: It's essential that you measure flour accurately when you bake. Use a spoon to lightly spoon the flour into the measuring cup, then level off the top. Never dip the measuring cup into the flour or you will add too much and your baked goods will be tough.

Apple Yogurt Parfait

Prep time: 15 minutes   **Cook time:** 10 minutes   **Serves 4**

Parfaits are a great idea for breakfast. Kids feel like they are eating dessert, but you know this recipe is good for you because it uses fresh fruit, yogurt for healthy probiotics, and granola bars for fiber. The apples in this version are briefly sautéed with sugar and cinnamon, then layered with Greek yogurt and crumbled granola bars for a delicious morning treat.

2 Granny Smith apples

2 teaspoons vegetable oil

2 tablespoons brown sugar

½ teaspoon ground cinnamon

3 chewy granola bars, crumbled

2 cups plain or vanilla Greek yogurt

1. Core the apples and cut into ½-inch pieces.

2. In a small saucepan, heat the oil over medium heat. Add the chopped apple, brown sugar, and cinnamon. Cook for 4 to 7 minutes, stirring frequently, until the apple is tender. Remove the apple mixture from the pan and put into a bowl and refrigerate for 5 minutes.

3. Meanwhile, crumble the granola bars and get your parfait glasses ready.

4. To assemble the parfaits, put about 1 tablespoon of crumbled granola bar into the bottom of each glass. Top with a few spoonfuls of yogurt and a spoonful of the apple mixture. Repeat this layering until you run out of ingredients.

5. Serve immediately or cover and chill for a few hours before serving.

Ingredient tip: For the fastest way to core an apple, place the apple upright on a cutting board. Use a sharp knife to cut down one side of the apple close to the core. Turn the apple a quarter turn and make another cut. Repeat until all of the apple is cut from the center section. Then chop the slices. Note that each time you turn the apple, the cut piece will be smaller.

Cranberry Cottage Bread

Prep time: 15 minutes   **Cook time:** 45 minutes   **Serves 6**

Cottage cheese is delicious in quick breads. The tangy flavor of the cheese adds interest, and this ingredient also makes the bread moist. The one thing about quick breads you need to know is: Do not overmix the batter or the bread will be tough; some lumps in the batter are fine. Slice this bread warm and spread with butter for a great breakfast.

Nonstick baking spray

**1¾ cups
   all-purpose flour**

**⅓ cup packed light
   brown sugar**

**1 teaspoon
   baking powder**

⅛ teaspoon salt

**½ cup small curd
   cottage cheese**

⅓ cup whole milk

**3 tablespoons
   butter, melted**

2 large eggs

⅓ cup dried cranberries

1. Preheat the oven to 350°F. Coat a loaf pan with baking spray and set aside.

2. In a large bowl, combine the flour, brown sugar, baking powder, and salt and set aside.

3. In a blender, combine the cottage cheese, milk, melted butter, and eggs. Blend until smooth.

4. Pour the cottage cheese mixture into the flour mixture and stir just until combined. Stir in the cranberries.

5. Spoon into the prepared pan. Bake for 40 to 50 minutes, or until a toothpick inserted into the center of the loaf comes out clean.

6. Let cool for 10 minutes in the pan on a rack, then turn the bread out of the pan onto the rack to cool.

Variation: You could substitute other dried fruits for the cranberries. Try chopped dried apricots, golden raisins, or dried currants. Or add some chopped pecans or walnuts instead of the dried fruit.

Baked French Toast Sandwiches

Prep time: 15 minutes **Cook time:** 40 minutes **Serves 6**

When I was a teenager, making French toast was my job on weekend mornings. I stood at the stove for quite a while, minding the toast and turning it as it cooked. I wish I had known about this recipe then! You just assemble a casserole, refrigerate it overnight, then pop it in the oven when you wake up. Serve with maple syrup or powdered sugar.

3 tablespoons butter, at room temperature

12 whole wheat bread slices

⅔ cup strawberry jam

1¼ cups whole milk

6 large eggs

¼ teaspoon salt

1. Grease the bottom of a 9-by-13-inch baking dish with the butter; use all of it.

2. Make 6 sandwiches with the bread and strawberry jam and put them into the baking dish in a single layer.

3. In a large bowl, combine the milk, eggs, and salt and beat until combined. Pour slowly over the bread in the casserole. Let stand for 5 minutes, then carefully flip each sandwich.

4. Cover with foil or plastic wrap and refrigerate for 8 hours or overnight.

5. In the morning, preheat the oven to 375°F.

6. Uncover the baking dish and bake for 40 to 50 minutes, until the bread is golden brown. Serve.

Variation: You can vary the filling in this recipe. Instead of a sweet recipe, try using cheese or ham (or both!) in place of the jam. Or you could use cream cheese or any type of sandwich spread.

Cranberry-Pear Baked Oatmeal

Prep time: 15 minutes   **Cook time:** 45 minutes   **Serves 8**

Baked oatmeal tastes like a cross between regular morning oatmeal and an oatmeal cookie. This super-easy recipe can be made the night before. Cover and refrigerate overnight, then bake in the morning. You'll love the texture and flavor of this warm breakfast treat. The pear baby food is a quick substitute for a peeled, cored, and chopped pear.

Nonstick baking spray

3 cups old-fashioned rolled oats

⅓ cup packed light brown sugar

1 teaspoon ground cinnamon

½ teaspoon baking soda

¼ teaspoon sea salt

1¼ cups whole milk

1 (4-ounce) jar pear baby food

2 large eggs

3 tablespoons butter, melted

1 cup dried cranberries

1. Preheat the oven to 375°F. Coat a 9-by-13-inch baking dish with baking spray and set aside.

2. In a large bowl, combine the oats, brown sugar, cinnamon, baking soda, and salt and mix. Add the milk, baby food, eggs, and melted butter and mix until combined. Stir in the cranberries.

3. Spoon the mixture into the prepared baking dish. You can cover the dish with plastic wrap and refrigerate at this point.

4. Bake for 40 to 50 minutes (adding another 5 to 10 minutes if the mixture was refrigerated), until the oatmeal is firm to the touch. Let cool for 5 minutes and serve.

Ingredient tip: Not all oatmeal is certified gluten-free because some are processed on the same lines that also process wheat. If you are avoiding gluten, read the label and make sure that the oats are gluten-free.

Variation: For a little more prep time, you can make baked oatmeal muffins. Just spoon the mixture into greased muffin tins, filling each cups about three-quarters full. Bake for 15 to 20 minutes, until firm. Unmold and serve warm.

Chewy Granola Bars

Prep time: 15 minutes   **Cook time:** 15 minutes   **Makes 20 bars**

Granola bars have been a go-to snack for decades. It's easy to buy granola bars, but making your own is cheaper, and the bars taste even better. These bars are rich with chocolate chips and nuts. This recipe makes a bunch, and they freeze really well.

Nonstick baking spray

3 cups old-fashioned rolled oats

2 cups crisp rice cereal

¾ cup whole wheat flour

½ cup packed light brown sugar

½ teaspoon sea salt

12 tablespoons (1½ sticks) butter, melted

¾ cup honey

⅓ cup almond butter

1 tablespoon vanilla extract

1 cup mini chocolate chips

1 cup chopped pecans

1. Preheat the oven to 350°F. Line a 9-by-13-inch baking dish with foil and coat the foil with baking spray. Set aside.

2. In a large bowl, combine the oats, cereal, flour, brown sugar, and salt and mix well. Add the melted butter, honey, almond butter, and vanilla and stir until thoroughly combined. Add the chocolate chips and pecans.

3. Press the mixture into the prepared pan, making sure to press firmly.

4. Bake the bars for 15 to 18 minutes, until the bars are set. Cool in the pan on a wire rack.

5. When cool, cut into 20 bars and wrap each in plastic wrap before storing in an airtight container at room temperature up to 5 days.

Variation: To make these bars gluten-free, substitute any commercially available gluten-free flour mix for the whole wheat flour.

Mini Egg and Veggie Bites

Prep time: 10 minutes   **Cook time:** 20 minutes   **Makes 12 bites**

Egg bites were made popular by a famous coffee chain. These little egg muffins are perfect for breakfast on the run, and they are so easy to make. You can use any left-over cooked vegetable in this recipe and choose your favorite type of cheese.

Nonstick cooking spray

9 large eggs

⅓ cup light cream

¼ teaspoon salt

⅛ teaspoon freshly ground black pepper

1 cup shredded Colby cheese

1 (4-ounce) jar sliced mushrooms, drained

3 tablespoons finely sliced scallions, both white and green parts

1. Preheat the oven to 375°F. Coat a silicone or metal 12-cup muffin tin with cooking spray. Set aside.

2. In a large bowl, beat the eggs with the cream, salt, and pepper.

3. Divide the cheese, mushrooms, and scallions among the prepared muffin cups.

4. Slowly pour the egg mixture over the vegetables and cheese in each muffin cup, filling about three-quarters full.

5. Bake for 18 to 22 minutes, until the egg bites are puffed and light golden brown. Cool for 5 minutes, then serve.

Cooking tip: If you want to freeze the egg bites, freeze them solid on a baking sheet or freezer-safe plate, then put into a plastic freezer bag. Let the egg bites thaw in the refrigerator overnight, then reheat in the microwave on high power for 20 to 30 seconds apiece.

Variation: If you want to use leftover cooked vegetables in these little egg cups, substitute ¾ cup of chopped cooked carrots, peas, chopped bell peppers, chopped asparagus, or corn in place of the jarred mushrooms. You could also use chopped cooked bacon or cooked crumbled sausage.

Veggie Frittata

Prep time: 15 minutes   **Cook time:** 35 minutes   **Serves 6**

A frittata is like an omelet but is much less delicate, so it's easier to make. This f
is baked in the oven. First, the vegetables are roasted, then the egg mixture is po
over and it's baked until puffy and golden brown. You can serve this frittata hot, at
room temperature, or even cold.

3 tablespoons butter, melted

12 asparagus stalks, cut into 1-inch pieces

1 red bell pepper, chopped

2 scallions, both white and green parts, sliced

12 large eggs

½ cup sour cream

½ teaspoon sea salt

⅛ teaspoon freshly ground black pepper

1½ cups shredded Swiss cheese

1. Preheat the oven to 375°F.
2. Drizzle the melted butter into a 9-by-13-inch baking dish. Add the asparagus, bell pepper, and scallions.
3. Roast for 7 to 9 minutes, until the vegetables are tender. Remove the pan from the oven but leave the oven on.
4. In a large bowl, combine the eggs, sour cream, salt, and pepper and beat well. Pour over the vegetables in the pan. Top evenly with the cheese.
5. Return to the oven and bake for 30 to 40 minutes, until the eggs are puffed and the frittata is golden brown. Cut into squares to serve.

Ingredient tip: To trim asparagus, hold the end of each spear and bend. It will naturally break at the point where the stem becomes too tough. Then rinse the asparagus well and slice or chop. You can save the tough bottoms for making soup.

...esy Potato Hash

...utes   **Cook time:** 15 minutes   **Serves 4**

...chopped potatoes, meat, and vegetables. It
...vers, but you can make this recipe with fresh
...id easy to make.

in a large skillet, heat the olive oil over medium heat.

2. Add the onion and cook for 3 to 4 minutes, stirring occasionally, until the onion is crisp-tender.

3. Add the hash browns and cook, again stirring occasionally, for 5 to 7 minutes, or until the potatoes begin to brown. Add the ham and stir.

4. Add the beaten eggs and stir gently until the eggs are cooked, about 4 minutes. Sprinkle with the cheese, remove the pan from the heat, cover, and let stand for a few minutes, or until the cheese melts. Serve.

...d
...rained
...d
...ed ham
...arge eggs, beaten
1 cup shredded Havarti or Swiss cheese

Ingredient tip: You can shred your own potatoes instead of using the refrigerated, prepared type, if you want. Just peel the potatoes and shred them directly into cold water. Squeeze the water out of the potatoes, dry in a kitchen towel, and use in the recipe. Or, use frozen shredded hash brown potatoes. Thaw them overnight in the refrigerator, then drain and proceed with the recipe.

Classic Blueberry Pancakes

Prep time: 15 minutes   **Cook time:** 10 minutes   **Makes 8 pancakes**

Pancakes are one of the first recipes beginning cooks learn to make. There are only two rules for making fluffy and tender pancakes: Measure the flour carefully and don't overmix the batter. This recipe has some ground oats for great texture and flavor.

⅓ cup old-fashioned rolled oats

1 cup all-purpose flour

3 tablespoons light brown sugar

1 teaspoon baking powder

⅛ teaspoon sea salt

1 cup light cream

1 large egg

1 large egg yolk

4 tablespoons (½ stick) butter, melted, divided

1 cup blueberries

1. In a blender, grind the oats until very finely ground.

2. In a large bowl, combine the oats with the flour, brown sugar, baking powder, and salt.

3. In a large glass measuring cup or medium bowl, combine the cream, whole egg, egg yolk, and 2 tablespoons of melted butter and mix until blended.

4. Stir the cream mixture into the flour mixture just until combined. There will be some lumps in the batter; that's just fine.

5. In a large skillet, melt the remaining 2 tablespoons of butter over medium heat.

6. Drop the batter by ⅓-cup measures into the skillet. Top each pancake with 8 to 10 blueberries.

7. Cook until small bubbles form on the tops of the pancakes and the edges look cooked, about 4 minutes. Carefully flip each pancake and cook for another 2 minutes, or until the bottoms are lightly browned.

8. Repeat with the remaining batter and blueberries.

Cooking tip: You can freeze pancakes for an instant breakfast on another day. Just freeze them individually, then place into freezer bags and freeze for up to 2 months. To reheat, microwave each frozen pancake for 20 to 25 seconds on high.

Spiced Maple Sausage Bake

Prep time: 15 minutes   **Cook time:** 40 minutes   **Serves 6**

This easy and elegant recipe starts with croissants and breakfast sausages. A touch of applesauce adds some tart sweetness. You make it the night before, then bake when you're ready to eat. Serve with more maple syrup and some crisp bacon.

Nonstick baking spray

8 large croissants, torn into pieces

1 (10-ounce) package fully cooked breakfast sausage, chopped

7 large eggs

½ cup light cream

⅓ cup sour cream

⅓ cup maple syrup

¼ cup applesauce

3 tablespoons light brown sugar

2 teaspoons vanilla extract

½ teaspoon ground cinnamon

⅛ teaspoon sea salt

1. Coat a 9-by-13-inch baking dish with baking spray. Arrange the croissants and chopped sausages in the baking dish in an even layer.

2. In a large bowl, combine the eggs, light cream, sour cream, maple syrup, applesauce, brown sugar, vanilla, cinnamon, and salt and beat until smooth. Pour into the pan over the croissants and sausages.

3. Cover and refrigerate overnight.

4. In the morning, preheat the oven to 350°F.

5. Uncover the pan and bake for 35 to 45 minutes, until the casserole is puffed and golden. Cut into pieces to serve.

Substitution: For a vegetarian option, you can omit the sausages. Instead, core and chop 2 Granny Smith apples and sauté in 1 tablespoon butter for 4 to 5 minutes, until tender. Combine with the croissants in the baking dish and add ½ cup chopped pecans. Proceed with the recipe.

Breakfast Pizza

Prep time: 15 minutes   **Cook time:** 15 minutes   **Serves 4**

A special weekend treat, this recipe takes all the things you love on your breakfast plate and puts them on a pizza base. Sausages and some veggies top the premade crust in this recipe, then beaten egg is drizzled over all. The pizza is baked until the eggs are set and the cheese is melted. Yum!

1 (12-inch) premade pizza crust

1 pound bulk sweet Italian sausage

1 onion, chopped

2 large eggs, beaten

⅛ teaspoon salt

⅛ teaspoon freshly ground black pepper

1½ cups shredded Cheddar cheese

1. Preheat the oven to 400°F.

2. Put the pizza crust onto a baking sheet and set aside.

3. In a large skillet, cook the sausage and onion over medium heat for 4 to 6 minutes, stirring occasionally, until the pork is fully cooked. Drain off the fat.

4. Spread the pork mixture evenly over the crust.

5. In a small bowl, beat the eggs with the salt and pepper until combined and drizzle over the pork. Top with the Cheddar.

6. Bake for 10 to 14 minutes, until the eggs are set and the cheese is melted and starting to brown. Cut into wedges to serve.

Ingredient tip: The best way to cut an onion is to first slice it from root to pointed top. Remove the outer skin. Place the onion cut-side down on a cutting board and cut into 6 slices. Then make cuts perpendicular to the first slices to make pieces. Make sure you curl the fingers that are holding the onion under so you don't cut yourself, and be sure to use a good, sharp knife.

Nut and Fruit Scones

Prep time: 15 minutes   **Cook time:** 20 minutes   **Makes 12 scones**

Scones are easy to make and fun to eat. Stir together a simple dough, pat it out into a round, cut into wedges, and bake. These are delicious eaten hot out of the oven or even days later. Warm them for 20 seconds each in the microwave, if you like.

1¾ cups all-purpose flour

⅓ cup packed light brown sugar

1½ teaspoons baking powder

¼ teaspoon salt

⅓ cup cold butter, cut into pieces

⅔ cup light cream, plus 1 tablespoon

1 large egg

⅓ cup chopped mixed nuts

¼ cup mixed dried fruit

1. Preheat the oven to 375°F. Line a baking sheet with parchment paper and set aside.

2. In a large bowl, combine the flour, brown sugar, baking powder, and salt and mix.

3. Using two knives or a pastry blender or your fingers, work the cold butter into the flour mixture until the particles of butter are about ⅛ inch in diameter.

4. In a small bowl, beat ⅔ cup of cream and the egg together. Add to the flour mixture and mix just until a dough forms. Add the nuts and fruit.

5. Gather up the dough, transfer to a floured surface, and knead 4 times. Form into an 8-inch disc and place on the prepared baking sheet.

6. Cut the dough into 8 wedges and separate slightly. Brush with the remaining 1 tablespoon of cream.

7. Bake for 15 to 20 minutes, until the scones are golden brown. Transfer the scones to a wire rack to cool for at least 10 minutes before serving.

Cooking tip: "Cutting" butter into flour is a technique used to make pastry dough. You just mix the butter into the flour until the butter is in small pieces. This makes the dough flaky when the butter melts in the dough in the oven. You can use your fingers, two knives, or a pastry blender, which is a tool that can be found in any supermarket.

Creamy Scrambled Eggs

Prep time: 10 minutes   **Cook time:** 10 minutes   **Serves 4**

The secret to the creamiest scrambled eggs is to cook them over low heat. Some cream added to the eggs makes them fluffy. You can serve these as is and they are delicious, but you could also add some cheese, cover the pan, and let it melt for a few minutes before serving.

9 large eggs

¼ cup sour cream

3 tablespoons heavy cream

⅛ teaspoon sea salt

⅛ teaspoon freshly ground black pepper

2 tablespoons butter

1. In a large bowl, beat the eggs with the sour cream, cream, salt, and pepper. Don't overbeat; just mix until the mixture is all one color.

2. In a large skillet, heat the butter over low heat until it melts.

3. Add the eggs all at once. Stir with a silicone spatula as the eggs start to set. Turn the eggs over and run your spatula across the bottom, lifting the eggs to let the uncooked portion flow to the bottom of the pan.

4. When the eggs are almost set, remove from the heat, cover, and let stand for 2 minutes to finish cooking, then serve.

Ingredient tip: Most people have learned to crack an egg on the side of a bowl. Research has shown that this method is more likely to leave broken pieces of eggshell in the eggs. What you should do is hold the egg firmly and give it a good tap on the counter, then hold it over the bowl and gently pull the egg apart. If some eggshell does get into the egg, use another piece of eggshell to get it out.

Succotash Salad,
page 32

CHAPTER THREE
Salads and Sides

Almost Instant Coleslaw

Prep time: 15 minutes   **Serves 6**

Coleslaw is a classic side dish at cookouts and barbecues. It's refreshing and crisp and takes just seconds to make. The secret is to buy coleslaw mix from the supermarket. That doesn't mean this coleslaw will be boring; you'll add some delicious ingredients to it, including a homemade dressing to take it to the next level.

1 (14-ounce) bag
   coleslaw mix

½ cup dried cranberries

2 tablespoons chopped
   fresh parsley

⅔ cup mayonnaise

2 tablespoons freshly
   squeezed lemon juice

2 tablespoons
   honey mustard

½ teaspoon celery salt

1. In a large bowl, combine the coleslaw mix, cranberries, and parsley and toss.

2. In a medium bowl, combine the mayonnaise, lemon juice, honey mustard, and celery salt and mix until smooth.

3. Pour over the coleslaw and toss to coat. Serve immediately or cover and chill for a few hours before serving. Store in the refrigerator.

Variation: You can make this recipe with cabbage you chop yourself, of course. Use a chef's knife, cut the cabbage in half, then cut out the solid core and slice. Turn the slices 45 degrees and cut again to make small pieces.

Easy Niçoise Salad

Prep time: 15 minutes   **Cook time:** 30 minutes   **Serves 4**

A Niçoise salad is a refreshing composed salad that comes from Nice on the Mediterranean coastline of France. "Composed" means the ingredients aren't mixed together but are arranged on a large serving platter in a beautiful way. To save time, this recipe uses baby potatoes and frozen green beans, along with canned tuna and olives.

1 pound baby potatoes

8 tablespoons olive oil, divided

3 tablespoons freshly squeezed lemon juice

1 teaspoon dried thyme leaves

¼ teaspoon salt

⅛ teaspoon freshly ground black pepper

1 (16-ounce) package frozen whole green beans

6 cups mixed salad greens

1 cup cherry tomatoes

1 (12-ounce) can white tuna, drained

4 store-bought hard-boiled eggs, sliced

16 pitted olives

1. Preheat the oven to 400°F.

2. Cut the baby potatoes in half and spread on a rimmed baking sheet. Toss with 1 tablespoon of olive oil. Roast for 20 to 25 minutes, until the potatoes are tender.

3. Meanwhile, in a large bowl, combine the remaining 7 tablespoons of olive oil, the lemon juice, thyme, salt, and pepper.

4. Microwave the green beans according to the package directions.

5. Add the salad greens and cherry tomatoes to the dressing in the bowl and toss.

6. To assemble the salad, place the greens and cherry tomatoes on a large platter. Top with the potatoes in one section, the green beans in another, and the tuna in another. Arrange the eggs around the platter, then sprinkle with the olives, and serve.

Ingredient tip: Most grocery stores carry hard-boiled eggs in the dairy section. If they don't, make them yourself. In a saucepan, cover the eggs with cold water and bring to a hard boil. Boil for 1 minute, then cover the pan, remove it from the heat, and let stand for 12 minutes. Put the eggs into ice water, let stand 5 minutes, then crack the eggs under the water so the water gets between the shell and the egg, and peel.

Mixed Green Salad with Ranch Dressing

Prep time: 15 minutes   **Serves 6**

Ranch salad dressing is simple to make, and the homemade version tastes even better than the purchased variety. Serve with a nice mix of several different lettuces for an instant side dish that's perfect with roast chicken or meatloaf.

4 ounces cream cheese, at room temperature

½ cup mayonnaise

⅓ cup whole milk

2 tablespoons freshly squeezed lemon juice

1 teaspoon dried parsley

1 teaspoon dried dill weed

¼ teaspoon onion powder

¼ teaspoon garlic powder

¼ teaspoon sea salt

⅛ teaspoon freshly ground black pepper

6 cups mixed salad greens

1. In a medium bowl, using a spoon, beat the cream cheese until soft. Gradually add the mayonnaise and mix until smooth. Beat in the milk and lemon juice.

2. Add the parsley, dill weed, onion powder, garlic powder, salt, and pepper and mix. Pour into a clean screw-top jar and refrigerate until needed.

3. To make the salad, put the greens in a serving bowl, drizzle with about ¼ cup of the dressing, toss gently, and serve. (Store the remaining dressing in the refrigerator for up to 1 week.)

Variation: If you omit the milk and all but 1 tablespoon of lemon juice, the dressing can become a delicious vegetable dip. Serve with baby carrots, celery strips, bell pepper slices, and cherry tomatoes.

Pesto Rice Salad

Prep time: 10 minutes   **Cook time:** 15 minutes   **Serves 6**

Though not as commonly used as pasta, rice makes a delicious base for a side salad. To make things easy, we start with frozen, cooked brown rice, then add a wonderfully creamy pesto dressing, along with a medley of veggies.

4 (10-ounce) packages frozen brown rice

1 (9-ounce) container basil pesto

⅓ cup mayonnaise

2 tablespoons freshly squeezed lemon juice

1 (10-ounce) package frozen peas, thawed

1 red bell pepper, chopped

3 scallions, both white and green parts, sliced

1. Cook the rice according to package directions.

2. Meanwhile, in a serving bowl, combine the pesto, mayonnaise, and lemon juice and mix until smooth.

3. Add the rice, peas, bell pepper, and scallions and mix gently.

4. Serve immediately or cover and chill for a few hours before serving.

Variation: If you add some cooked shrimp or chopped chicken breast to this recipe, you can serve this as a main-dish salad.

Succotash Salad

Prep time: 15 minutes   **Cook time:** 10 minutes   **Serves 6**

Succotash is an all-American side dish made of corn and lima beans or butter beans. This recipe turns it into a savory and fresh salad when paired with cherry tomatoes and avocado. Add the avocado just before serving so it stays nice and green.

1 (16-ounce) package frozen corn kernels

1 (16-ounce) package frozen lima beans

1 cup cherry tomatoes

¼ cup olive oil

2 tablespoons red wine vinegar

1 tablespoon Dijon mustard

¼ teaspoon sea salt

⅛ teaspoon freshly ground black pepper

1 avocado, halved, peeled, and cubed

1. Cook the corn and lima beans using the microwave directions on their respective packages. Drain well and transfer to a large bowl.

2. Add the cherry tomatoes and toss.

3. In a small bowl, combine the olive oil, vinegar, mustard, salt, and pepper and mix well. Pour over the salad and toss.

4. Cover and chill for a few hours. When ready to serve, add the avocado and toss.

Variation: In the summer, you can use fresh corn instead of frozen, but the preparation time will be longer. Cook 4 ears of corn for 3 minutes in boiling water, then let cool for a bit. Then cut off the kernels with a sharp knife. If you can find them, fresh green soybeans (edamame) are delicious in this recipe, and don't require cooking.

Quinoa Veggie Salad

Prep time: 15 minutes   **Cook time:** 15 minutes   **Serves 6**

Quinoa is a seed that is unusual because it provides complete protein. It has a nutty taste and wonderful texture. Make sure that you rinse quinoa before you cook it because it has a bitter coating. Once rinsed and cooked, this seed is made into a delicious and colorful salad.

2 cups vegetable broth

1 cup quinoa

⅓ cup olive oil

3 tablespoons freshly squeezed lemon juice

3 tablespoons chopped fresh flat-leaf parsley

½ teaspoon sea salt

⅛ teaspoon freshly ground black pepper

2 cups frozen corn kernels, thawed

1 red bell pepper, chopped

2 scallions, both green and white parts, sliced

1. Place the quinoa in a fine-mesh sieve and rinse thoroughly with cool water until the water runs clear.

2. In a medium saucepan, combine the vegetable broth and quinoa. Bring to a simmer over medium heat, then reduce the heat to low and simmer, covered, for 12 to 15 minutes, until the quinoa is tender.

3. In a salad bowl, combine the olive oil, lemon juice, parsley, salt, and black pepper and mix well.

4. Add the quinoa, corn, bell pepper, and scallions and toss to coat.

5. Serve immediately or cover and chill for a few hours before serving. Store leftovers in the refrigerator.

Variation: To make this into a main-dish salad, you can add a can of drained chickpeas or some chopped cooked chicken or shrimp.

Cobb Salad

Prep time: 15 minutes   **Cook time:** 10 minutes   **Serves 6**

A Cobb salad is a traditional salad composed of romaine lettuce, chicken, avocado, tomatoes, and a savory dressing. This recipe combines all those ingredients in a tossed salad that's easier to make and serve.

6 bacon slices

⅓ cup olive oil

3 tablespoons red wine vinegar

2 tablespoons Dijon mustard

¼ teaspoon sea salt

⅛ teaspoon freshly ground black pepper

1 (18-ounce) bag hearts of romaine lettuce

2 cups cubed cooked chicken breast (see tip)

1½ cups cherry tomatoes

1 avocado, halved, peeled, and cubed

1. In a skillet, cook the bacon over medium heat for 8 to 10 minutes, turning several times, until crisp. Drain the bacon on paper towels and crumble. Remove the bacon grease from the pan, reserving 1 tablespoon of the bacon drippings.

2. In a salad bowl, combine the reserved bacon drippings, the olive oil, vinegar, mustard, salt, and pepper and blend well.

3. Add the lettuce, chicken, tomatoes, and bacon and toss thoroughly to coat.

4. Top with the avocado and serve.

Ingredient tip: You can use leftover cooked chicken breast, buy precooked chicken breasts from the store, or cook your own. To cook your own, in a saucepan, combine 2 raw chicken breasts and 2 cups water and bring to a simmer. Simmer over low heat, partially covered, for 10 minutes, then remove the pan from the heat, cover, and let stand for 20 minutes, or until the chicken registers 165°F on an instant-read thermometer. Cool and chop.

Loaded Baked Potato Salad

Prep time: 15 minutes   **Cook time:** 50 minutes   **Serves 6**

Real potato salad is a lot of work. You have to boil potatoes, let them cool a bit, peel them, then cut into chunks. Just the hands-on time to prepare the potatoes is about half an hour. So, we are going to bake the potatoes instead. Cut them in half, scoop out the flesh, and mix with the dressing. Done!

6 large russet potatoes

1 tablespoon olive oil

¾ cup mayonnaise

¼ cup whole milk

3 tablespoons yellow mustard

1 cup cubed Colby cheese

6 bacon slices, cooked and crumbled

3 scallions, both white and green parts, chopped

1. Preheat the oven to 400°F.

2. Scrub the potatoes, pierce each with a fork, and dry. Rub with the olive oil.

3. Put the potatoes directly on the oven rack. Bake for 45 to 55 minutes, until fork-tender. Remove the potatoes from the oven and cool for 15 minutes on a wire rack.

4. Meanwhile, in a large bowl, combine the mayonnaise, milk, and mustard and mix well. Add the cheese, bacon, and scallions.

5. When the potatoes have cooled a bit, cut each half lengthwise and scoop out the flesh directly into the dressing. Mix gently but thoroughly.

6. Serve immediately or cover and chill for a few hours before serving.

Ingredient tip: Don't throw away the potato skins! Cut each potato skin in half lengthwise and place on a baking sheet. Top with shredded Cheddar cheese, cooked crisp bacon, scallions, and bake at 400°F for 10 to 15 minutes, until the skins are crisp. Serve with sour cream.

Classic Scalloped Potatoes

Prep time: 15 minutes   **Cook time:** 1 hour 15 minutes   **Serves 6 to 8**

Potatoes do take some time to prepare, especially for scalloped potatoes. You have to peel them and slice them thinly. This recipe avoids all that work and just uses frozen shredded potatoes baked in a creamy sauce.

1 (32-ounce) package frozen hash brown potatoes

3 garlic cloves, minced

1 (8-ounce) package cream cheese, cubed

1 cup heavy cream

1 cup light cream

1. Arrange the potatoes in an even layer in a 9-by-13-inch baking dish and sprinkle with the garlic.

2. In a microwave-safe medium bowl, combine the cream cheese, heavy cream, and light cream. Microwave for 1 minute, then stir. Continue microwaving in 1-minute intervals, stirring after each, until the mixture is smooth.

3. Pour the cream cheese mixture over the potatoes and mix gently.

4. Bake for 30 minutes, then stir. Bake for another 30 minutes and stir again. Finally, bake for 15 to 20 minutes longer, until the potatoes are tender and the casserole is bubbling and starting to brown on top. Serve.

Variation: You can use frozen diced potatoes, sometimes called Southern-style hash browns, in place of the shredded potatoes. Increase the baking time by 10 to 15 minutes.

Creamy Mashed Potatoes

Prep time: 15 minutes   **Cook time:** 15 minutes   **Serves 6 to 8**

Mashed potatoes are true comfort food, and everyone should know how to make them. But most recipes tell you to peel and cube potatoes, then boil them until tender, and this takes a long time. This recipe uses diced frozen potatoes that are boiled, then mashed with cream and butter, for a much easier version.

1 (24-ounce) package frozen diced potatoes

4 tablespoons (½ stick) butter

1 cup light cream

⅓ cup sour cream

½ teaspoon sea salt

⅛ teaspoon freshly ground black pepper

1. Bring a large pot of water to a boil. Add the frozen diced potatoes. Bring the water back to a boil, then reduce the heat and simmer for 10 to 15 minutes, until the potatoes are soft.

2. Drain the potatoes and return them to the hot pan. Cook over low heat for 1 to 2 minutes, stirring constantly, until the steaming stops to dry the potatoes.

3. Remove the pot from the heat and add the butter. Use a potato masher to mash the potatoes. Beat in the light cream, sour cream, salt, and pepper until smooth. Serve.

Variation: You can dress up these mashed potatoes by adding other ingredients, such as crisp bacon, chopped scallions, or shredded cheese.

Herbed Garlic Bread

Garlic bread is a must anytime you serve anything Italian. It's delicious with spaghetti and lasagna. It's also a fabulous accompaniment to soups and stews. This bread is laden with garlic and herbs on a crisp, soft bread. The mayonnaise is unconventional but a delicious addition.

1 loaf French bread, halved horizontally

⅓ cup butter, melted

2 tablespoons mayonnaise

4 garlic cloves, minced

3 tablespoons minced fresh parsley

2 teaspoons minced fresh thyme leaves

1. Preheat the oven to 350°F.
2. Place the two halves of the French bread cut-side up on a baking sheet.
3. In a small bowl, combine the melted butter, mayonnaise, garlic, parsley, and thyme and mix well. Spread this mixture evenly on the cut sides of the bread.
4. Bake for 15 to 20 minutes, until the bread is light golden brown on top. Cut into slices to serve.

Ingredient tip: Most cooks in the know make grilled cheese sandwiches spread with mayonnaise on the outside instead of butter for perfectly browned results. The mayo does the same thing for this garlic bread and adds a great tangy flavor, too.

Roasted Honey Sweet Potatoes with Pecans

Prep time: 10 minutes **Cook time:** 35 minutes **Serves 6**

Many people make sweet potatoes only at Thanksgiving, and that's a shame. My husband doesn't like sweet potatoes, so when he was going to graduate school and had meetings at night, I would often roast a sweet potato and have it for dinner using a recipe similar to this one. This recipe is a great side dish for everything from meatloaf to grilled steak. The potatoes roast until they are tender and brown and crisply glazed.

1 (16-ounce) bag cubed sweet potatoes

¼ cup honey

2 tablespoons butter

1 tablespoon olive oil

½ teaspoon sea salt

⅛ teaspoon freshly ground black pepper

1 cup small pecan halves

1. Preheat the oven to 400°F.
2. Arrange the sweet potato cubes in a single layer on a rimmed baking sheet.
3. In a small saucepan, combine the honey, butter, olive oil, salt, and pepper and heat over low heat for a few minutes until the butter melts and the mixture is smooth.
4. Pour the honey mixture over the sweet potatoes and toss to coat.
5. Roast for 20 to 25 minutes, until the potatoes are almost tender.
6. Add the pecans to the potatoes and toss gently. Roast for another 8 to 12 minutes, until the pecans are darker brown and the potatoes are tender. Serve.

Variation: You can substitute cubed squash such as pumpkin, acorn squash, or butternut squash for the sweet potatoes. The cooking time will be the same. These vegetables are often available already cut up at the grocery store.

Chipotle Roasted Brussels Sprouts

Prep time: 10 minutes   **Cook time:** 20 minutes   **Serves 6**

Yes, yes, I know, many people hate Brussels sprouts. I did, too. I used to hide them in my pockets at dinner when I was young. But now I love them, and when they are roasted they become gloriously sweet and tender with crunchy edges. Some chipotle peppers add a nice kick to this delicious side dish.

1½ pounds Brussels sprouts

2 tablespoons garlic-infused olive oil

2 tablespoons chopped chipotle peppers in adobo sauce

¼ teaspoon sea salt

⅛ teaspoon freshly ground black pepper

1. Preheat the oven to 400°F.
2. Trim the bottoms off each Brussels sprout and cut each in half. Place them on a rimmed baking sheet as you work.
3. Drizzle the Brussels sprouts with the garlic oil, then sprinkle with the chipotle peppers, salt, and black pepper and toss. Arrange in a single layer.
4. Roast for 20 minutes, or until the Brussels sprouts are tender and golden brown around the edges. Serve.

Ingredient tip: Chipotle peppers are smoked jalapeño peppers. They are sold packed in a spicy sauce called adobo. You can use the peppers, the sauce, or both in any recipe for a good level of heat.

Ingredient tip: Garlic-infused olive oil is an easy kitchen short-cut that can provide your dishes with the flavor of garlic while saving a bit on prep time. Look for it where olive oil is sold in the grocery store.

Creamed Spinach

Prep time: 15 minutes   **Cook time:** 15 minutes   **Serves 6**

Creamed spinach is a classic old-fashioned steakhouse recipe that's easy to make if you start with a bag of frozen cut-leaf spinach. Add some cheese, a white sauce, and garlic, and your spinach will be ready to eat in about 30 minutes.

1 (16-ounce) bag frozen cut-leaf spinach

4 tablespoons (½ stick) butter

3 garlic cloves, minced

3 tablespoons all-purpose flour

½ teaspoon sea salt

⅛ teaspoon freshly ground black pepper

1¼ cups light cream

1 cup grated Havarti cheese

1. In a colander, rinse the spinach with cool water and leave to drain.

2. Meanwhile, in a medium saucepan, melt the butter over medium heat. Add the garlic and cook and stir for 1 minute.

3. Sprinkle the flour, salt, and pepper into the garlic mixture and cook for 2 to 3 minutes, stirring with a wire whisk, until the mixture bubbles.

4. Add the light cream and stir with a whisk until blended. Simmer for 3 to 4 minutes, stirring occasionally, to thicken.

5. Wrap the spinach in a dry kitchen towel and press or squeeze to remove excess liquid.

6. Stir the Havarti into the sauce until melted, then add the spinach and bring just to a simmer. Serve.

Ingredient tip: You must buy frozen cut-leaf spinach packaged in a bag for this recipe. Don't buy the spinach frozen in a block, because the pieces are smaller and you'll spend quite some time separating the bits of spinach.

Classic Chicken
Noodle Soup, page 45

CHAPTER FOUR
Soups, Chilis, and Stews

Broccoli Cheese Soup

Prep time: 15 minutes   **Cook time:** 15 minutes   **Serves 4**

Most broccoli cheese soups have the same ingredients: butter, onion, broccoli, cheese, and milk. This one adds beer for a wonderful malty flavor. You can use nonalcoholic beer if you'd like.

4 tablespoons (½ stick) butter

1 onion, chopped

2 celery stalks, sliced

2 garlic cloves, minced

¼ cup all-purpose flour

2 cups vegetable broth or chicken stock

1 (12-ounce) can beer

2 cups broccoli florets

1½ cups shredded Cheddar cheese

1 cup light cream

1. In a large saucepan, melt the butter over medium heat. Add the onion, celery, and garlic and cook for 3 minutes, stirring, until beginning to soften. Add the flour and stir for 2 minutes.

2. Add the broth and beer, bring to a simmer, and simmer for 2 minutes. Add the broccoli florets and simmer for 4 to 5 minutes, stirring occasionally, until the broccoli is tender.

3. Stir in the Cheddar and cream until the cheese is melted. Do not boil. Serve hot.

Variation: Instead of the beer, you can use more chicken stock or vegetable broth. If you do omit the beer, add 1 tablespoon Dijon mustard along with the cheese for more flavor.

Classic Chicken Noodle Soup

Prep time: 15 minutes   **Cook time:** 40 minutes   **Serves 4**

Chicken noodle soup is the ultimate comfort food. It is the best thing to eat when you have a cold; there is scientific evidence that proves it can make you feel better. This version is super simple to make because it uses boneless cubed chicken and chicken stock, instead of stewing a whole chicken. Serve it with garlic bread or some cheese crackers.

2 tablespoons butter

1 tablespoon olive oil

6 boneless, skinless chicken thighs, cubed

½ teaspoon sea salt

⅛ teaspoon freshly ground black pepper

1 onion, chopped

3 garlic cloves, minced

4 cups chicken stock

1 (16-ounce) package baby carrots

1 bay leaf

1½ cups fine egg noodles

1 teaspoon dried thyme leaves

1. In a large saucepan, heat the butter and olive oil over medium heat. Add the chicken, sprinkle with the salt and pepper, and cook for about 4 minutes, stirring occasionally, until the chicken starts to brown.

2. Remove the chicken from the saucepan and set aside. Add the onion and garlic to the pan drippings in the saucepan and cook for 3 minutes, stirring occasionally.

3. Return the chicken to the saucepan and add the chicken stock, carrots, and bay leaf. Bring to a simmer, reduce the heat to low, and simmer for 20 minutes, or until the vegetables are tender. Discard the bay leaf.

4. Add the egg noodles and thyme to the pan and simmer for 8 to 10 minutes, until the chicken is thoroughly cooked and the noodles are tender. Serve hot.

Cooking tip: Pan drippings are the bits of fat and meat left in a pan after meat has been browned. These little bits have lots of flavor and should be incorporated into the soup or sauce you're making. You may need to scrape the bottom of the pan with a spoon to release all the drippings.

Lentil Soup

A classic dish that has stood the test of time, lentil soup is simple to make and so good for you. Lentils are high in fiber and contain compounds that can protect against cancer and heart disease. This version combines veggies with the lentils and adds herbs and some tomato paste for great flavor.

2 tablespoons olive oil

1 onion, chopped

3 garlic cloves, minced

6 cups vegetable broth

1 (16-ounce) package baby carrots

2 cups Puy lentils, rinsed and picked over

3 tablespoons tomato paste

½ teaspoon sea salt

⅛ teaspoon freshly ground black pepper

1 tablespoon freshly squeezed lemon juice

1 teaspoon dried thyme leaves

½ teaspoon dried oregano leaves

1. In a large saucepan or a stockpot, heat the olive oil over medium heat. Add the onion and garlic and cook for 3 to 4 minutes, stirring occasionally, until softened.

2. Add the vegetable broth, carrots, lentils, tomato paste, salt, and pepper and bring to a simmer. Reduce the heat to low and simmer for 25 to 35 minutes, until the lentils are soft.

3. Stir in the lemon juice, thyme, and oregano and simmer for a few minutes longer. Serve hot.

Ingredient tip: There are several types of lentils you can buy. Puy lentils are grown in France and are a blue-green color with a rich and peppery flavor. Brown lentils are the most common, with an earthy flavor. And red lentils are sold skinned and split, so they cook quickly and are usually used as a thickener. Always sort through lentils before using because there may be some small pebbles in the bag.

Ingredient tip: Buy tomato paste in a tube and you can add 1 or 2 tablespoons to any recipe without having to open a can. Store the tomato paste in the refrigerator.

Garlic Chicken Barley Soup

Prep time: 15 minutes   **Cook time:** 15 minutes   **Serves 6**

This is one of my favorite winter recipes because it's so comforting and rich. Barley is a great grain to use in soup: It's nutty and tender and is really good for you because it's high in fiber and can help control blood sugar levels. Barley is combined with chicken, garlic, and other veggies in this hearty and homey soup. Serve with a green salad and some garlic toast for a great dinner.

2 tablespoons garlic-infused olive oil

3 boneless, skinless chicken breasts, cubed

1 onion, chopped

4 garlic cloves, minced

½ teaspoon sea salt

⅛ teaspoon freshly ground black pepper

6 cups chicken stock

2 cups frozen corn kernels

1 (14.5-ounce) can diced tomatoes, undrained

1 cup quick-cooking barley

½ teaspoon poultry seasoning

1 tablespoon freshly squeezed lemon juice

1. In a large saucepan or a stockpot, heat the garlic oil over medium heat. Add the chicken, onion, and garlic and stir, scraping up the pan drippings as they form. Sprinkle with the salt and pepper and cook for 3 minutes, or until the vegetables are crisp-tender.

2. Add the chicken stock, corn, tomatoes and their juices, barley, and poultry seasoning and bring to a simmer. Reduce the heat to low and simmer for 11 to 14 minutes, until the barley is tender and the chicken is thoroughly cooked.

3. Stir the lemon juice into the soup and serve hot.

Ingredient tip: There are several types of barley available in stores. Hulled barley is minimally processed and is the most nutritious. Pearl barley has some of the bran removed, so the cooking time is shorter, about 40 minutes. And quick-cooking barley is processed further so it cooks in about 10 minutes.

Classic Minestrone

Prep time: 15 minutes   **Cook time:** 55 minutes   **Serves 6**

A hearty favorite, minestrone is an Italian soup heavy on the vegetables and made with beans and macaroni. It really is a complete meal in a pot. To save time, preshredded cabbage, sliced mushrooms, and canned beans are used. Top this soup with some grated Parmesan and serve with garlic bread.

2 tablespoons olive oil

1 onion, chopped

4 garlic cloves, minced

6 cups chicken stock

1 (16-ounce) package baby carrots

2 cups preshredded cabbage

1 (15-ounce) can cannellini beans, drained and rinsed

1 (14.5-ounce) can diced tomatoes, undrained

1 teaspoon Italian seasoning

½ teaspoon sea salt

⅛ teaspoon freshly ground black pepper

1 bay leaf

1 cup elbow macaroni

½ cup shredded Parmesan cheese

1. In a large saucepan or stockpot, heat the olive oil over medium heat. Add the onion and garlic and cook for 3 to 5 minutes, stirring occasionally, until crisp-tender.

2. Add the chicken stock, carrots, cabbage, beans, tomatoes and their juices, Italian seasoning, salt, pepper, and bay leaf. Bring to a simmer, then reduce the heat to low and simmer for 30 to 40 minutes, until the vegetables are tender.

3. Stir in the macaroni, bring to a simmer, and simmer for 8 to 10 minutes, until the pasta is tender.

4. Discard the bay leaf, then stir in the Parmesan and serve hot.

Variation: There are so many different vegetables that can be used in minestrone. Think about adding green beans, frozen peas, chopped zucchini or summer squash, winter squash cubes, celery, kale, spinach, or collard greens.

Creamy Pea Soup

Prep time: 15 minutes   **Cook time:** 15 minutes   **Serves 4**

This super-simple soup can be served hot or cold. It's a perfect make-ahead recipe to have chilled on a hot summer day, and it's warming and comforting on a winter night. Mint adds a fresh note. Keep the ingredients for this soup on hand for an easy meal.

2 tablespoons butter

1 (16-ounce) bag frozen peas

4 cups chicken stock or vegetable broth

1 tablespoon freshly squeezed lemon juice

½ teaspoon sea salt

¼ teaspoon dried mint leaves

⅛ teaspoon freshly ground black pepper

⅓ cup sour cream

1. In a large saucepan or a stockpot, melt the butter over medium heat. Add the peas and cook for 1 minute. Add the stock, lemon juice, salt, mint, and pepper and bring to a simmer. Simmer for 13 to 16 minutes, until the peas are very tender.

2. Transfer the soup, in batches, to a blender and blend until smooth. Add the sour cream to the last blender batch. Pour the batches back into the saucepan.

3. You can either reheat the soup (don't let it boil) or chill the soup for a few hours until cold. If necessary, thin out the chilled soup with more stock or broth before serving.

Substitution: You can use fresh mint leaves instead of the dried mint in this recipe. Here's the general rule for substituting fresh herbs for dried: Use three times the amount of fresh as dried. In this recipe you would add about ¾ teaspoon minced fresh mint.

Ham and Corn Chowder

Prep time: 10 minutes   **Cook time:** 15 minutes   **Serves 4**

A chowder is a soup that has been thickened with flour or cornstarch. It's considered heartier than a soup and can serve as the whole meal. This recipe is a classic—salty ham and sweet corn are perfect partners. Use frozen corn for ease of preparation, but in the summer, you can substitute fresh corn cut off the cob, if you'd like.

1½ cups chopped ham

1 onion, chopped

2 tablespoons butter

3 garlic cloves, minced

4 cups vegetable broth

1 (16-ounce) package frozen corn kernels

1 teaspoon dried basil

1½ cups light cream

2 tablespoons cornstarch

1. In a large saucepan or a stockpot, combine the ham, onion, butter, and garlic. Cook over medium heat for 3 to 4 minutes, stirring occasionally, until the onion is crisp-tender.

2. Add the broth, corn, and basil and bring to a simmer. Reduce the heat to low and simmer for 6 to 8 minutes, until the corn is tender.

3. In a small bowl, combine the cream and cornstarch and whisk together. Stir into the soup and simmer for 2 to 3 minutes to thicken the soup. Serve hot.

Ingredient tip: If you have leftover ham, use it here, but if not, look for chopped ham at any deli and in the meat section of the supermarket.

Cooking tip: Stock and broth are two different things. Stock is made with bones, such as chicken or beef bones, while broth is made without bones. Vegetable broth is always broth.

Fragrant Thai-Style Shrimp Soup

Prep time: 15 minutes   **Cook time:** 15 minutes   **Serves 4**

This simple soup takes just minutes to prepare and cook. The ingredients reminiscent of Thai food include ginger, lime juice, coconut milk, baby corn, and cilantro. Serve the soup with a fresh fruit salad.

1 pound medium shrimp, peeled and deveined

3 cups vegetable broth

1 (13.5-ounce) can full-fat coconut milk

1 (8-ounce) can baby corn, drained

1 teaspoon ground ginger

2 tablespoons freshly squeezed lime juice

1 tablespoon chopped fresh cilantro

1. In a large saucepan, combine the shrimp, broth, coconut milk, corn, and ginger and bring to a simmer over medium heat. Then stir, reduce the heat to low, and simmer for 8 to 12 minutes, until the shrimp curls and turn pink.

2. Stir in the lime juice and cilantro and serve hot.

Ingredient tip: You can usually buy shrimp that have been peeled and deveined. If you can't, pull the shells off the shrimp, then cut a slit along the back and discard the dark vein running down the center. Shrimp is sold by the number per pound. Medium shrimp are usually about 40 count per pound, while large shrimp are 30 count per pound.

Clam and Veggie Chowder

Prep time: 15 minutes **Cook time:** 25 minutes **Serves 6**

Clam chowder is the ultimate comfort food. This version is filled with bacon, cream, and lots of frozen veggies to cut down on preparation time. It's creamy and cheesy and the perfect choice for a cold winter night.

4 bacon slices

1 onion, chopped

3 tablespoons all-purpose flour

½ teaspoon sea salt

⅛ teaspoon freshly ground black pepper

2 cups frozen diced potatoes

2 cups vegetable broth or clam juice

1 cup frozen sliced carrots

1 cup frozen corn

1 bay leaf

2 cups light cream

2 (6-ounce) cans chopped clams, drained

1 cup shredded Swiss cheese

1. In a large saucepan or a stockpot, cook the bacon over medium heat, turning several times, for 8 to 10 minutes, until crisp. Transfer the bacon to paper towels to drain, then crumble and set aside.

2. Add the onion to the bacon drippings in the pan and cook for 3 minutes, or until crisp-tender. Add the flour, salt, and pepper and cook for 2 minutes.

3. Add the potatoes, broth, carrots, corn, and bay leaf and bring to a simmer. Reduce the heat to low and simmer for 8 to 10 minutes, until the vegetables are tender.

4. Discard the bay leaf. Stir in the cream, clams, and Swiss cheese and stir well.

5. Increase the heat to medium and cook for 3 to 5 minutes, until the soup is steaming and the cheese is melted. Don't let it boil. Serve topped with the bacon.

Ingredient tip: Canned clams are already cooked, so they don't need to be cooked in the soup; you are just reheating them. Add them at the end of cooking time and never boil them.

Chicken Pasta Stew

Prep time: 15 minutes **Cook time:** 25 minutes **Serves 6**

A stew is the heartiest of all soups. It is thick with vegetables, meats, and pasta, and makes a delicious dinner when served with garlic toast and a green salad. This colorful stew is no exception, bringing plenty of flavor with the addition of herbs and cheese.

2 tablespoons butter

1 (8-ounce) package sliced mushrooms

1 onion, chopped

1 cup sliced celery

5 cups chicken stock

2 cups baby carrots

½ teaspoon sea salt

⅛ teaspoon freshly ground black pepper

3 cups cubed cooked chicken

⅔ cup orzo pasta

1 teaspoon dried basil

1 (8-ounce) package cream cheese, cubed

1. In a large saucepan or a stockpot, melt the butter over medium heat. Add the mushrooms, onion, and celery and cook, stirring, for 4 minutes, or until the onion is crisp-tender.

2. Add the chicken stock, carrots, salt, and pepper and bring to a simmer. Simmer for 8 to 10 minutes, until the vegetables are tender.

3. Add the chicken, orzo, and basil and simmer for another 7 to 9 minutes, until the pasta is tender.

4. Add the cream cheese and cook for another 3 to 5 minutes, stirring, until the cheese is melted and the soup is creamy. Serve hot.

Ingredient tip: There are many varieties of sliced mushrooms available at most grocery stores. For this recipe, you can use button mushrooms or try baby portabella (also called cremini mushrooms) for more flavor.

Ingredient tip: Orzo pasta is shaped like grains of rice. It cooks quickly and will help thicken stews and soups if you cook the pasta right in the stew.

Wild Rice Chili

Prep time: 15 minutes   **Cook time:** 50 minutes   **Serves 6**

There is a raging controversy about chili. Some people, especially those from Texas, insist that chili should never contain beans. Then there are other people who think it's not chili unless there are beans! I am in the latter camp; it's not chili to me unless there are some beans. This hearty recipe complicates things further because it uses wild rice, too. Oh well—just enjoy it!

1 pound lean ground beef

1 onion, chopped

3 garlic cloves, minced

4 cups beef stock

1 (15-ounce) can black or kidney beans, drained and rinsed

1 (14.5-ounce) can diced tomatoes, undrained

⅔ cup wild rice, rinsed

1 tablespoon chili powder

½ teaspoon sea salt

⅛ teaspoon cayenne pepper

1. In a large saucepan or a stockpot, cook the ground beef with the onion and garlic, stirring to break up the meat, for 4 to 5 minutes, until the beef is browned.

2. Add the beef stock, beans, tomatoes and their juices, wild rice, chili powder, salt, and cayenne and bring to a simmer. Reduce the heat to low and simmer for 40 to 50 minutes, stirring occasionally, until the wild rice is tender. Serve hot.

Ingredient tip: Wild rice isn't actually a rice, but a grass seed. It is grown in wetlands in the upper Midwest. When you buy it, look for long grains that aren't broken.

Baked Meatball Stew

Prep time: 15 minutes   **Cook time:** 2 hours   **Serves 6**

Ordinarily, a recipe like this would take about 45 minutes to prepare. But we are using a few convenience foods that really speed up prep time. And the stew is still rich and deeply flavored, full of vegetables and herbs. This is a long-cooking recipe good for cozy winter weekends.

2 tablespoons olive oil

1 (8-ounce) package sliced cremini mushrooms

1 onion, chopped

3 cups beef stock

2 cups frozen diced potatoes

2 large carrots, sliced

1 (16-ounce) package frozen meatballs

1 (14.5-ounce) can diced tomatoes, undrained

2 teaspoons dried parsley

1 teaspoon dried marjoram leaves

1. Preheat the oven to 375°F.

2. In a large Dutch oven (or other ovenproof lidded pot), heat the olive oil over medium heat. Add the mushrooms and onion and cook, stirring, for 5 minutes, or until tender.

3. Add the beef stock, potatoes, carrots, meatballs, tomatoes and their juices, parsley, and marjoram and stir.

4. Cover, transfer to the oven, and bake for 1¾ to 2 hours, until the meatballs are hot, the vegetables are tender, and the stew is thick. Serve hot.

Cooking tip: Dutch ovens are large and heavy ovenproof pots with close-fitting lids. They are usually made of cast iron, and some have an enamel coating. They can be expensive, but you can find good ones for around $40. A Dutch oven will last a lifetime if well cared for.

Beef Burgundy Stew

Prep time: 15 minutes   **Cook time:** 2 hours   **Serves 6**

To make this comfort classic, beef is stewed with red wine and all kinds of vegetables to make a rich and delicious dinner. This recipe is simmered on the stovetop in a soup pot or Dutch oven. Most of the ingredients are already prepared when you buy them, so there is very little prep time for a stew this complex. This is definitely a meal in one; all you need is a glass of wine.

1½ pounds cubed beef stew meat

3 tablespoons all-purpose flour

½ teaspoon salt

⅛ teaspoon freshly ground black pepper

2 tablespoons olive oil

1 (8-ounce) package sliced mushrooms

1 onion, chopped

1 pound baby potatoes

3 cups beef stock

1 (16-ounce) package baby carrots

1 cup red Burgundy wine

3 tablespoons tomato paste

1 bay leaf

1. In a bowl, toss the meat with the flour, salt, and pepper to coat.

2. In a large stockpot or Dutch oven, heat the olive oil over medium heat. Add the meat and brown for 5 minutes, turning occasionally. Remove the meat from the pot and set aside.

3. Add the mushrooms and onion to the pot and brown for 5 minutes, scraping up the pan drippings. Return the meat to the pot along with the potatoes, beef stock, carrots, wine, tomato paste, and bay leaf and stir.

4. Bring to a simmer, then reduce the heat to low and simmer for 1½ to 2 hours, stirring once or twice, until the meat and vegetables are tender. Discard the bay leaf before serving.

Ingredient tip: You can often find cubed stew meat at the grocery store, but you can also buy a chuck roast and ask the butcher to cube it for stew. Most stores will do this for no extra charge.

Ingredient tip: When you buy wine for cooking, always buy a wine that you would drink. Poor quality or cheap wine will ruin a recipe. If you don't want to use the wine, just add another cup of beef stock.

Irish Stew

Prep time: 15 minutes   **Cook time:** 1 hour 30 minutes   **Serves 6**

Irish stew is a very old-fashioned recipe with traditional ingredients. It's rich and thick and typically made with some type of beer, along with chunks of tender pork, potatoes, and carrots. Serve it with warm scones or soda bread from the bakery.

1½ pounds pork shoulder, cut into 1½- to 2-inch cubes

3 tablespoons all-purpose flour

½ teaspoon sea salt

⅛ teaspoon freshly ground black pepper

2 tablespoons olive oil

1 onion, chopped

1 pound baby potatoes

1 (16-ounce) package baby carrots

2 cups beef broth

1 (12-ounce) bottle malty beer

½ teaspoon caraway seeds

1. In a bowl, toss the pork with the flour, salt, and pepper.

2. In a large stockpot or Dutch oven, heat the olive oil over medium heat. Add the pork and brown, stirring occasionally, for about 5 minutes. Remove the pork from the pot.

3. Add the onion to the pot and stir for a couple of minutes to release the pan drippings. Add the potatoes, carrots, broth, beer, and caraway seeds. Return the pork to the pot.

4. Bring to a simmer, then cover the pot, reduce the heat to low, and simmer for 1 hour 30 minutes, or until the vegetables and pork are tender. Serve hot.

Cooking tip: To prepare meat for stews and soups, cut off and discard excess fat, but leave some fat on, because that's where the flavor is.

Butternut Squash and
Veggie Lasagna, page 63

CHAPTER FIVE
Vegetarian Mains

Baked Mac and Cheese

Prep time: 15 minutes   **Cook time:** 1 hour 15 minutes   **Serves 4**

Mac and cheese is a classic vegetarian main dish and one of my favorite recipes. I have experimented with many versions, and this is the easiest and my favorite. This version starts with uncooked macaroni in a lot of liquid. It's baked in the oven, so the macaroni has a marvelous texture because the dairy products slow down the water absorption. You'll love this comforting recipe.

2 tablespoons butter, at room temperature

3 cups whole milk

1 cup light cream

2¼ cups elbow macaroni

2 cups shredded Colby cheese

2 cups shredded Swiss cheese

1. Preheat the oven to 350°F.

2. Using all of the butter, coat the bottom and 1 inch up the sides of a 9-by-13-inch baking dish. Pour the milk and cream into the dish. Add the macaroni and the Colby cheese and stir gently.

3. Cover the pan with foil, transfer to the oven, and bake for 30 minutes.

4. Uncover and gently stir the mixture, making sure to scrape the bottom. Cover again and bake for another 25 minutes.

5. Uncover the pan and add the Swiss cheese and stir. Leave uncovered and bake for 15 to 20 minutes longer, until the pasta is tender, the mixture is bubbling, and it starts to brown on top. Serve hot.

Variation: For a lower-fat version, reduce the butter to 1 tablespoon. Use 2 percent milk in place of the whole milk and use whole milk in place of the light cream.

Vegetable Fried Rice

Prep time: 15 minutes   **Cook time:** 10 minutes   **Serves 6**

Fried rice is a wonderfully satisfying and simple dish to make at home, but there's one trick: You have to start with cold cooked rice. There are several ways to do this. You can cook rice and refrigerate some for this recipe. You can buy rice at a restaurant. Or you can thaw frozen cooked rice. Whichever method you choose, this recipe is quick and delicious.

2 tablespoons garlic-infused olive oil

1 onion, chopped

2 (10-ounce) packages frozen white or brown rice, thawed

1 cup frozen baby peas

2 large eggs, beaten

1 cup baby spinach leaves

2 tablespoons reduced-sodium soy sauce

2 tablespoons vegetable broth

1. In a large skillet or a wok, heat the garlic oil over medium-high heat. Add the onion and stir-fry for about 3 minutes, or until crisp-tender.

2. Add the rice and peas and stir-fry for 2 minutes.

3. Add the eggs and stir-fry for 2 minutes, or until the eggs are set. Add the spinach, soy sauce, and broth and stir-fry for 2 to 3 minutes longer to heat through. Serve.

Cooking tip: When you are stir-frying food, you have to keep the food moving pretty constantly or it will be unevenly cooked. Use a heatproof spatula; it can be made of silicone or metal. Just keep adding the food and stirring and dinner will be ready in no time.

Baked Two-Cheese Sandwiches

Prep time: 15 minutes   **Cook time:** 10 minutes   **Serves 6**

Yes, you can bake grilled cheese sandwiches, and they will be delicious and crisp, with gooey melted cheese. This trick seems impossible, but it does work! Just be aware that when you turn the sandwiches, they will not look done. But I promise that when you take them out of the oven, they will be perfectly cooked.

6 tablespoons (¾ stick) butter, at room temperature

¼ cup mayonnaise

12 slices sturdy white or whole wheat bread

1½ cups shredded Cheddar cheese

1 cup shredded provolone cheese

1. Preheat the oven to 425°F.

2. In a small bowl, combine the butter and mayonnaise and beat well. Spread this mixture onto one side of each bread slice. Place the half of the bread slices coated-side down on a rimmed baking sheet.

3. In a bowl, combine the cheeses and toss. Divide the cheeses among the bread slices. Top with the remaining slices, coated-side up.

4. Bake the sandwiches for 5 minutes, then carefully turn with a spatula. Bake for another 4 to 6 minutes, until the sandwiches are golden brown. Serve.

Variation: Add other ingredients to these sandwiches. Try a spoonful of basil pesto or some chopped chipotles in adobo sauce or spread some cream cheese on the insides of the bread before you add the shredded cheese. You could also add mashed avocado or some sliced scallions.

Butternut Squash and Veggie Lasagna

Prep time: 15 minutes   **Cook time:** 1 hour 15 minutes   **Serves 6**

Lasagna can be very time-consuming to make, what with chopping vegetables, shredding cheese, and cooking the noodles, not to mention assembling. This version is much easier because it uses no-boil noodles, precut veggies, and preshredded cheese. But it still has all the great richness and depth of flavor you expect from lasagna.

Nonstick cooking spray

2 tablespoons olive oil

2 cups cubed butternut squash

1 (8-ounce) package sliced cremini mushrooms

2 cups baby spinach

1 (26-ounce) jar pasta sauce

1 cup part-skim ricotta cheese

1 cup full-fat cottage cheese

2 large eggs

1 teaspoon Italian seasoning

1 (9-ounce) package no-boil lasagna noodles

2 cups shredded mozzarella cheese

½ cup grated Parmesan cheese

1. Preheat the oven to 375°F. Coat a 9-by-13-inch baking dish with cooking spray and set aside.

2. In a large skillet, heat the olive oil over medium heat. Add the squash and cook for 5 minutes, stirring occasionally, until almost tender. Add the mushrooms and cook, stirring occasionally, for 5 to 6 minutes, until the mushrooms give up their liquid and the liquid evaporates. Add the spinach and stir for 2 minutes, or until wilted. Add the pasta sauce and bring to a simmer.

3. Meanwhile, in a medium bowl, combine the ricotta cheese, cottage cheese, eggs, and Italian seasoning and beat well.

4. Put about ½ cup of the pasta sauce mixture in the bottom of the prepared baking dish. Top with a layer of noodles. Add one-third of the ricotta cheese mixture, one-third of the mozzarella, and then one-third of the remaining pasta sauce mixture.

5. Repeat the layers, ending with the pasta sauce. Sprinkle with the Parmesan.

6. Cover the pan with foil and bake for 50 minutes to 1 hour, until the noodles are tender when pierced with a fork. Let stand for 10 minutes, then cut into squares to serve.

Variation: You can use many other vegetables in this easy and versatile recipe. Try chopped zucchini or summer squash, sliced green beans, onions, garlic, or bell peppers.

Classic Cheese Quiche

Prep time: 15 minutes   **Cook time:** 30 minutes   **Serves 4**

A quiche can easily take an hour to prepare if you make the crust from scratch. Omit the crust and this recipe is quick and easy to make. Lots of veggies add color, flavor, and interest.

Nonstick baking spray

1 tablespoon olive oil

1 cup sliced mushrooms

1 cup broccoli florets

8 large eggs

⅓ cup whole milk

½ teaspoon dried
   thyme leaves

½ teaspoon salt

⅛ teaspoon freshly
   ground black pepper

1 cup shredded
   Muenster cheese

2 tablespoons grated
   Parmesan cheese

1. Preheat the oven to 350°F. Coat a 9-inch square baking dish with baking spray and set aside.

2. In a medium skillet, heat the olive oil over medium heat. Add the mushrooms and cook for 4 minutes, stirring occasionally. Add the broccoli and cook for another 2 minutes, stirring occasionally. Spread the vegetables over the bottom of the prepared baking dish.

3. In a large bowl, beat the eggs with the milk, thyme, salt, and pepper until combined. Pour into the baking dish. Top with the Muenster and Parmesan cheeses.

4. Bake for 25 to 35 minutes, until the egg mixture is puffed and starting to brown. Cut into squares to serve.

Variation: If you do want to make a quiche with a crust, reduce the eggs to 6. Use the No-Roll Pie Crust (page 120) and fit it into a 9-inch pie pan. Bake the quiche for 35 to 40 minutes, until set.

Unstuffed Cabbage

Prep time: 15 minutes   **Cook time:** 15 minutes   **Serves 4**

Stuffed cabbage is a classic German recipe that typically takes a lot of preparation. This recipe uses all the ingredients for stuffed cabbage, but in an "unstuffed" form so it's a lot easier to make. The end result is rich, fragrant, and truly satisfying.

1 tablespoon olive oil

1 onion, chopped

3 garlic cloves, minced

2 (10-ounce) packages frozen brown rice, thawed

1 (14.5-ounce) can diced tomatoes, undrained

1 (14-ounce) package coleslaw mix

3 tablespoons tomato paste

2 tablespoons Dijon mustard

1 tablespoon honey

1 teaspoon dried marjoram leaves

1. In a large skillet, heat the olive oil over medium heat. Add the onion and garlic and cook for 2 to 4 minutes, stirring occasionally, until crisp-tender.

2. Add the brown rice, tomatoes and their juices, coleslaw mix, tomato paste, mustard, honey, and marjoram and bring to a simmer. Reduce the heat to low and simmer for 8 to 11 minutes longer, until the cabbage is tender. Serve.

Ingredient tip: Coleslaw mix typically is a combination of shredded cabbage and carrots. You can use either green or red cabbage for this recipe. The shredded cabbage cooks more quickly than chopped fresh cabbage, so this recipe cooks in 15 minutes.

Two-Bean Burritos

This classic Tex-Mex recipe can be served two ways: with the spicy bean mixture simply rolled up in tortillas and served as is, or covered in sauce and baked. This recipe is the first version. Most of the minimal prep time here is just rolling the tortillas.

1 tablespoon olive oil

1 onion, chopped

1 (16-ounce) can refried beans

1 (16-ounce) can kidney beans or black beans, drained and rinsed

1 cup frozen corn kernels

1 tablespoon chili powder

12 (6-inch) corn tortillas

1½ cups shredded pepper Jack cheese

1. In a large skillet, heat the oil over medium heat. Add the onion and cook for 2 minutes, or until crisp-tender. Stir in the refried beans, kidney beans, corn, and chili powder and simmer for 5 minutes.

2. Soften the tortillas as directed on the package and put them on a work surface.

3. Divide the bean filling among the tortillas, divide the cheese on top of the bean filling, then roll up and serve.

Variation: To bake the tortillas before serving, preheat the oven to 375°F. Arrange the filled tortillas in a greased baking pan in a single layer, cover with one 10-ounce can of enchilada sauce, and top with 1 cup of cheddar or pepper Jack cheese. Cover with foil and bake for 20 to 25 minutes, until hot. Or, fry them in a large skillet over medium heat in a few tablespoons of oil, turning frequently, until browned and crisp.

Portabella Stroganoff

Prep time: 15 minutes   **Cook time:** 15 minutes   **Serves 4**

Portabella mushrooms are large mushrooms that are great for stuffing with chopped vegetables and other fillings. They also make a wonderful meaty-tasting substitute for ground beef. Serve this rich stroganoff over hot cooked pasta, mashed potatoes, or rice.

1 tablespoon garlic-infused olive oil

1 onion, chopped

2 (12-ounce) packages portabella mushrooms, chopped

2 cups vegetable broth

1 tablespoon regular or vegan Worcestershire sauce

1 tablespoon reduced-sodium soy sauce

½ cup sour cream

2 tablespoons tomato paste

2 tablespoons all-purpose flour

⅛ teaspoon freshly ground black pepper

1. In a large skillet, heat the garlic oil over medium heat. Add the onion and cook for 2 minutes, stirring occasionally, until crisp-tender.

2. Add the mushrooms and cook for another 4 minutes. Add the broth, Worcestershire sauce, and soy sauce and bring to a simmer. Simmer for 7 to 8 minutes, until the mushrooms are tender.

3. In a small bowl, combine the sour cream, tomato paste, flour, and pepper and mix well. Add a spoonful of the liquid from the skillet and blend. Stir this mixture into the skillet and simmer for another 2 to 3 minutes to thicken the mixture. Serve.

Variation: If you can't find portabella mushrooms, you can substitute chopped button mushrooms in this recipe. Just cook the mushrooms in step 2 until they are browned for richer flavor; this can take up to 15 minutes.

Huevos Rancheros

Prep time: 15 minutes   **Cook time:** 15 minutes   **Serves 6**

This classic Mexican recipe has become an American staple. It's traditionally quite spicy, but you can adjust the heat level to your taste simply by adjusting the amount of red pepper flakes and jalapeños. The traditional version can take some time to make, but this version cuts some corners to make it very easy.

2 tablespoons olive oil

1 jalapeño
   pepper, minced

6 large eggs

¼ teaspoon sea salt

⅛ teaspoon red
   pepper flakes

3 cups tortilla chips,
   slightly crushed

1 (16-ounce) can
   refried beans

1¼ cups salsa

1½ cups shredded
   pepper Jack cheese

1 avocado, halved,
   peeled, and cubed

1. Preheat the oven to 400°F.

2. In a medium skillet, heat the olive oil over medium heat. Add the jalapeño and cook for 2 minutes.

3. Meanwhile, in a bowl, beat the eggs with the salt and pepper flakes.

4. Add the eggs to the skillet and cook for 3 to 4 minutes, stirring occasionally, until the eggs are just set. Remove from the heat.

5. Spread the tortilla chips in the bottom of a 9-by-13-inch baking dish. Drop the refried beans over the chips in dollops. Top with the salsa. Add the scrambled eggs to the baking dish by the spoonful. Then sprinkle with the pepper Jack.

6. Bake for 15 to 18 minutes, until the cheese is melted and starting to brown. Serve garnished with the avocado.

Ingredient tip: To mince a jalapeño, halve it lengthwise and take off the stem. Be careful with the seeds and membranes; that's where the heat is. You can remove the seeds or leave them in for more heat.

Ingredient tip: To cut an avocado, cut it in half lengthwise around the pit. Twist the avocado to separate the two halves. Hold the half with the pit in a towel to protect your hand and hit the pit with the blade of a large knife; the pit should come out attached to the blade. Use a large spoon to scoop the flesh out of each half, then slice, cube, or chop.

Broccoli Pasta Alfredo

Prep time: 15 minutes   **Cook time:** 15 minutes   **Serves 4**

This super-simple one-pot recipe is perfect for nights when you are so tired you'd rather order a pizza. It is literally made in one pot so there's very little cleanup. And all you do is just keep adding ingredients to the pot!

4 cups vegetable broth

1 (16-ounce) package gemelli or ziti pasta

⅛ teaspoon freshly ground black pepper

2 cups broccoli florets

½ cup heavy cream

½ cup part-skim ricotta cheese

½ cup grated Parmesan cheese, divided

1. In a large saucepan, combine the broth, pasta, and pepper and bring to a boil over high heat. Reduce the heat to medium and cook for 5 minutes.

2. Add the broccoli florets and cook, stirring occasionally, for 4 minutes longer.

3. Add the cream, ricotta, and ¼ cup of Parmesan and cook, stirring for 2 to 3 minutes longer, until the sauce starts to thicken and the pasta and broccoli are tender.

4. Serve sprinkled with the remaining ¼ cup of Parmesan.

Ingredient tip: You can often find prepared broccoli florets in the produce aisle of the supermarket. If not, buy a head of broccoli. Cut off the stems, then break the florets into smaller pieces. You can discard the stems or peel and chop them and add to stir-fries.

Cheesy Artichoke-Spinach Pizza

Prep time: 15 minutes   **Cook time:** 15 minutes   **Serves 4**

This pizza is based on the popular artichoke-spinach appetizer dip. It's super simple to make; just top a premade pizza crust (your own or purchased) and bake. It's faster than ordering pizza delivery! And much tastier.

1 (12-inch) premade pizza crust

¼ cup sour cream

¼ cup mayonnaise

1 (13-ounce) can artichoke hearts, drained and chopped

1 cup baby spinach

1½ cups shredded provolone cheese

3 tablespoons grated Parmesan cheese

1. Preheat the oven to 450°F.

2. Set the pizza crust on a baking sheet. Dollop the crust with the sour cream and mayonnaise and spread evenly. Top with the artichokes, spinach, provolone, and Parmesan.

3. Bake for 13 to 16 minutes, until the pizza crust is golden brown and the cheese is melted and starting to brown. Cut into wedges to serve.

Cooking tip: You may have heard of pizza stones. They are round and flat discs made of clay that are heated in the oven and make pizza crusts super crisp. If you want to use one, put it in the oven before you turn it on. Let the oven heat as long as the stone instructions say, then put the pizza directly on the stone using a large spatula or pizza peel.

Chickpea Curry

Prep time: 15 minutes   **Cook time:** 30 minutes   **Serves 6**

Chickpeas, also called garbanzo beans, are a great meat substitute. They have a slightly chewy texture and nutty taste and are delicious when combined with ingredients for curry. Coconut milk adds creaminess, and curry powder, garlic, and ginger add intense flavor. Serve over hot cooked brown rice.

1 tablespoon olive oil

1 onion, chopped

3 garlic cloves, minced

2 teaspoons curry powder

½ teaspoon ground ginger

½ teaspoon sea salt

⅛ teaspoon freshly ground black pepper

2 (15-ounce) cans chickpeas, drained and rinsed

1 (14.5-ounce) can diced tomatoes, undrained

1 (13.5-ounce) can full-fat coconut milk

1 (12-ounce) package fresh broccoli florets

⅓ cup water

2 tablespoons cornstarch

1. In a large saucepan, heat the olive oil over medium heat. Add the onion and garlic and cook for 3 minutes, stirring occasionally, until crisp-tender.

2. Add the curry powder, ginger, salt, and pepper and simmer for 1 minute, or until fragrant.

3. Add the chickpeas, tomatoes and their juices, and coconut milk and bring to a simmer. Simmer for 10 minutes, stirring occasionally.

4. Stir in the broccoli and simmer for 3 to 5 minutes longer, until the broccoli is crisp-tender.

5. In a small bowl, stir the water into the cornstarch. Stir into the curry and simmer for 2 to 3 minutes longer to thicken the sauce. Serve.

Ingredient tip: When you open a can of coconut milk, it will appear to be solid. This is just a layer of coconut cream that floats to the top of coconut milk when it sits. Use both the thick top part and the thinner bottom part in this recipe.

Veggie Risotto

Prep time: 15 minutes   **Cook time:** 40 minutes   **Serves 4**

Risotto is a time-consuming recipe; you have to stand at the stove and stir it for 20 to 25 minutes. But not if the risotto is baked in the oven! This neat trick makes creamy and suave risotto without all the work. This recipe is packed full of delicious veggies.

2 tablespoons olive oil

1 (8-ounce) package sliced mushrooms

1 onion, chopped

2 garlic cloves, minced

1 cup Arborio rice

½ teaspoon sea salt

⅛ teaspoon freshly ground black pepper

6 cups vegetable broth

2 cups frozen baby peas

1 cup halved cherry tomatoes

½ cup grated Parmesan cheese

1. Preheat the oven to 400°F.

2. In a large, heavy ovenproof skillet with a tight-fitting lid, heat the olive oil over medium heat for 1 minute. Add the mushrooms, onion, and garlic and cook for 4 minutes, stirring occasionally, until softened.

3. Add the rice and sprinkle with the salt and pepper. Cook, stirring, for 2 minutes longer. Add the broth and bring to a simmer. Cover the skillet with heavy-duty foil and top with the lid.

4. Transfer the skillet to the oven and bake for 20 minutes.

5. Remove the skillet from the oven, remove the lid and foil, and stir. Add the peas and tomatoes and cover with just the lid.

6. Return to the oven and bake for 7 to 10 minutes longer, until the rice is tender but still slightly firm in the middle. Stir in the Parmesan and serve.

Ingredient tip: Arborio rice is a special type of short-grain rice grown in Italy. It has more of a specific type of starch called amylopectin, which is branched (a reference to its structure, which means the starch is more soluble); cooking the rice in liquid releases the starch, which forms a gel and thickens the liquid.

Roasted Chicken and
Vegetables, page 82

CHAPTER SIX
Poultry and Seafood Mains

Chicken Cacciatore

Prep time: 15 minutes   **Cook time:** 1 hour 30 minutes   **Serves 4**

Cacciatore means "hunter" in Italian. And meat prepared "hunter style" originally meant cooked with herbs and onions. Tomatoes were added later when they were brought from the New World in the mid-16th century. This flavorful and hearty dish is easy to make; serve it over gluten-free pasta or rice.

1½ pounds boneless, skin-on chicken thighs

1 teaspoon dried thyme leaves

½ teaspoon garlic salt

⅛ teaspoon freshly ground black pepper

2 tablespoons garlic-infused olive oil

1 onion, chopped

3 garlic cloves, minced

1 (20-ounce) can crushed tomatoes

⅔ cup chicken broth

3 tablespoons tomato paste

1 cup red or yellow cherry tomatoes

¼ cup sliced pitted Kalamata olives

½ cup grated Romano cheese

1. Sprinkle the chicken with the thyme, garlic salt, and pepper.

2. In a large skillet, heat the garlic oil over medium heat. Add the chicken, skin-side down, and cook for 3 to 4 minutes, until the skin is browned.

3. Remove the chicken from the pan and set aside. Add the onion and garlic and cook, stirring occasionally, for 5 to 6 minutes, until the onion is tender.

4. Add the crushed tomatoes, chicken broth, and tomato paste and bring to a simmer. Add the chicken, cherry tomatoes and olives. Reduce the heat to low and simmer for 10 to 15 minutes, until the chicken registers 165°F and the juices run clear when you cut into it.

5. Sprinkle with the Romano before serving.

Variation: You can make this recipe with cubed boneless, skinless chicken breasts, too. The cooking time in step 4 decreases to 8 to 10 minutes.

Lemon Roast Chicken with Garlic

Prep time: 15 minutes   **Cook time:** 1 hour 30 minutes   **Serves 4**

Lemon and garlic are the best partners for tender roasted chicken. This recipe is perfect for Sunday lunch or entertaining. Serve it with mashed potatoes and cooked green beans for a classic dinner.

1 whole roasting chicken (3 to 4 pounds)

2 lemons

4 garlic cloves, smashed and peeled, divided

2 tablespoons butter, at room temperature

1 teaspoon sea salt

⅛ teaspoon freshly ground black pepper

1. Pat the chicken dry. Don't rinse it or you may spray bacteria around your kitchen.

2. Cut one of the lemons in half and put one half in the bird's cavity. Put three of the garlic cloves into the cavity.

3. Mince the remaining garlic clove. Slice the other lemon half into ¼-inch-thick slices. Grate 1 teaspoon lemon zest from the remaining lemon. Squeeze the juice from the lemon into a bowl.

4. In a small bowl, combine the butter, lemon zest, and minced garlic and mix well.

5. Loosen the skin over the chicken breast and spread half of the butter mixture underneath. Pull the skin back gently over the chicken and pin in place with toothpicks.

6. Drizzle the outside of the bird with the lemon juice, then rub with the remaining butter mixture. Sprinkle with the salt and pepper.

7. Arrange the lemon slices in the bottom of a 9-by-13-inch baking dish and put the bird breast-side up on top of the lemon slices.

8. Roast the chicken for 1 hour 30 minutes to 1 hour 40 minutes, until the leg moves freely in the joint, the juices run clear, and an instant-read thermometer registers 165°F. Let stand for 10 minutes before carving, then serve.

Cooking tip: To smash garlic cloves, put them on the work surface and use the side of a chef's knife to crush the clove. You can easily remove the garlic skin after doing this.

Chicken Parmesan Sandwiches

Chicken Parmesan is an entrée made with flattened chicken breasts, coated with bread crumbs (Parmesan cheese in this case), and sautéed until tender. Put that chicken in a hoagie roll and add some pasta sauce and cheese for a hearty and easy sandwich.

4 small boneless, skinless chicken breasts (4 ounces each)

1 teaspoon Italian seasoning

½ teaspoon salt

⅛ teaspoon freshly ground black pepper

1 large egg, beaten

1 cup grated Parmesan cheese

2 tablespoons olive oil

4 hoagie rolls or Italian rolls, split and toasted

4 slices mozzarella cheese

½ cup pasta sauce, warmed

1. Put the chicken breasts between sheets of wax paper or parchment paper and pound until about ¼ inch thick. Sprinkle with the Italian seasoning, salt, and pepper.

2. Dip each chicken breast into the egg, then into the Parmesan to coat.

3. In a large skillet, heat the oil over medium heat. Add the chicken and cook, turning once, for 3 to 4 minutes on each side until the chicken is golden brown and cooked through.

4. Make sandwiches with the split rolls, chicken, mozzarella, and pasta sauce and serve.

Variation: Turn the chicken Parmesan into a salad. When the chicken is done, cut into strips and toss with romaine hearts, olives, and sun-dried tomatoes and drizzle with Italian salad dressing.

Chicken Pot Pie

Prep time: 15 minutes   **Cook time:** 1 hour 30 minutes   **Serves 6**

This homey and comforting classic chicken pot pie recipe is perfect for a cold winter day or whenever you feel in need of some comfort. Puff pastry is used for the crust to make things easy and quick.

4 tablespoons (½ stick) butter

1 onion, chopped

¼ cup all-purpose flour

1 teaspoon poultry seasoning

1½ cups chicken broth

1 cup light cream

2 cups frozen mixed vegetables

2 cups shredded cooked chicken (see tip)

1 cup frozen shredded hash brown potatoes

Half a 9-by-15-inch sheet frozen puff pastry, thawed

1. Preheat the oven to 400°F.

2. In a large saucepan, melt the butter over medium heat. Add the onion and cook, stirring occasionally, until tender, about 4 minutes.

3. Add the flour and poultry seasoning and stir for 2 minutes until bubbling. Add the broth and cream and cook, stirring with a wire whisk, for 2 minutes. Add the vegetables, chicken, and potatoes and bring to a simmer.

4. Pour the mixture into a 9-inch square baking dish. Top with the puff pastry, gently pressing the edges of the pastry to the edges of the dish. Cut a few slits in the pastry.

5. Bake for 40 to 50 minutes, until the pastry is golden brown and the chicken mixture is bubbling.

Ingredient tip: To always have cooked chicken on hand, either roast a chicken or buy a rotisserie chicken or two from the supermarket. Remove the meat and shred, package in 2-cup portions in freezer bags, and freeze up to 3 months. One whole chicken should yield about 4 cups of shredded chicken.

Curried Chicken and Rice

Prep time: 10 minutes   **Cook time:** 20 minutes   **Serves 4**

Making a curry from scratch with traditional spices can be a lengthy process, but this Americanized version uses some time-saving workarounds to produce a mild and delicious sauce with lots of flavor.

2 tablespoons butter

2 tablespoons all-purpose flour

1 tablespoon curry powder

½ teaspoon sea salt

4 boneless, skinless chicken breasts, cubed

1 onion, chopped

1 cup chicken broth

½ cup heavy cream

⅓ cup mango chutney

2 cups sugar snap peas

2 (10-ounce) packages frozen brown rice, cooked according to package directions

1. In a large saucepan, heat the butter over medium heat until melted.

2. Meanwhile, in a medium bowl, combine the flour, curry powder, and salt and toss the chicken in this mixture.

3. Add the chicken along with any remaining flour mixture to the butter in the pan. Cook for about 4 minutes, stirring occasionally, until the chicken is light brown. It will not be fully cooked.

4. Remove the chicken from the pan. Add the onion to the pan and cook, stirring to release any pan drippings, for 4 minutes, or until the onion is tender. Stir in the broth, cream, and chutney and simmer for a few minutes.

5. Return the chicken to the pan and simmer for 5 minutes. Add the snap peas and simmer for another 2 to 3 minutes, until the chicken is cooked through and the peas are tender. The juices will run clear and the chicken will be white inside when it is done.

6. Serve over the brown rice.

Ingredient tip: Mango chutney is a sauce made from mangoes, raisins, ginger, garlic, and lots of spices. It's slightly sweet and very flavorful. Major Grey is the most popular brand of this chutney, but there are many other brands. Have a taste test to discover which one is your favorite.

Sloppy Janes

Prep time: 10 minutes   **Cook time:** 20 minutes   **Serves 6**

Sloppy Janes are sloppy Joe sandwiches that are made with ground chicken or turkey instead of ground beef. They are a bit lighter in taste but are still rich and delicious. Serve on whole wheat hamburger buns or hoagie rolls that have been toasted to stand up to the rich sauce.

2 tablespoons olive oil

1 onion, chopped

1 cup preshredded carrots

1 pound ground turkey or chicken

1 teaspoon poultry seasoning

⅛ teaspoon freshly ground black pepper

1 (8-ounce) can tomato sauce

2 tablespoons ketchup

2 tablespoons yellow mustard

4 hamburger buns, split and toasted

1. In a large saucepan, heat the olive oil over medium heat. Add the onion and carrots and cook for about 4 minutes, stirring occasionally, until tender.

2. Add the ground turkey, poultry seasoning, and pepper. Cook for about 5 minutes, stirring occasionally to break up the meat, until the meat is cooked.

3. Add the tomato sauce, ketchup, and mustard and bring to a simmer. Simmer for 3 to 4 minutes to thicken the mixture a bit.

4. Serve on the hamburger buns.

Variation: You can use other vegetables in this recipe. Try sliced mushrooms, chopped bell peppers, or even corn or peas. By the way, this is a great recipe to get kids to eat more veggies.

Roasted Chicken and Vegetables

Prep time: 15 minutes   **Cook time:** 35 minutes   **Serves 4**

One pan dinners are a tired cook's best friend. You just plop all of the ingredients in a pan and bake. That's it. And there are infinite variations on this recipe. Make this with sausages, pork chops, chicken thighs, or go vegetarian and sprinkle some feta or blue cheese over the veggies just before serving.

8 bone-in, skin-on chicken thighs

1 pound baby Yukon Gold potatoes, halved

2 cups baby carrots

1 onion, sliced

8 garlic cloves, unpeeled

2 tablespoons olive oil

1 tablespoon freshly squeezed lemon juice

1 teaspoon Italian seasoning

½ teaspoon sea salt

⅛ teaspoon freshly ground black pepper

1. Preheat the oven to 400°F. Line a rimmed baking sheet with parchment paper or foil.

2. Put the chicken, potatoes, carrots, onion, and garlic on the pan. Drizzle with the oil and lemon juice and sprinkle with the Italian seasoning, salt, and pepper. Toss to coat, then arrange everything in a single layer.

3. Roast for 30 to 40 minutes, until the vegetables are tender and the chicken reads 165°F on an instant-read thermometer. The juices will run clear when the chicken is done.

Ingredient tip: When garlic cloves are roasted whole in their skins, they become very tender, soft, and sweet. Squeeze them out of the skins and gobble them up.

Chicken Blueberry Corn Salad

Prep time: 15 minutes   **Serves 4**

There are about as many chicken salad recipes on the planet as there are chickens. This recipe is special because it combines some ingredients you wouldn't expect, but they work. The sweetness of the blueberries and corn complement each other. And the color is beautiful.

⅓ cup olive oil

2 tablespoons freshly squeezed lemon juice

2 tablespoons honey

2 tablespoons Dijon mustard

1 teaspoon dried thyme leaves

½ teaspoon sea salt

⅛ teaspoon freshly ground pepper

4 ears of corn

4 cups shredded cooked chicken breast

2 cups blueberries

1 cup cubed Colby cheese

3 scallions, both white and green parts, chopped

1. In a large bowl, combine the olive oil, lemon juice, honey, mustard, thyme, salt, and pepper and whisk to combine.

2. Cut the kernels off the corn cobs and add to the dressing.

3. Add the chicken, blueberries, cheese, and scallions and mix gently.

4. Serve immediately or cover and refrigerate for a few hours before serving.

Ingredient tip: Cutting corn off the cob takes a bit of practice, but it's easy once you get the hang of it. I found the best way is to put one end of the cob in the hole in a Bundt pan. Cut down the sides of the cob and the kernels will fall into the pan. If you can't find fresh corn, substitute 2 cups cooked frozen corn.

Orange Chicken

Prep time: 15 minutes   **Cook time:** 25 minutes   **Serves 6**

A favorite on Chinese-takeout menus, orange chicken marries deep-fried chicken chunks with a spicy sauce made with orange juice. Deep-frying is messy and takes too much time, so this chicken is baked in the oven before it's mixed with the flavorful sauce. Serve over hot cooked brown rice for a great meal.

4 boneless, skinless chicken breasts, cubed

⅛ teaspoon cayenne pepper

2 large eggs, beaten

2 cups orange juice, divided

1 cup plain dried bread crumbs

⅓ cup orange marmalade

2 tablespoons reduced-sodium soy sauce

2 tablespoons cornstarch

1 teaspoon ground ginger

½ teaspoon garlic powder

1. Preheat the oven to 425°F. Line a baking sheet with parchment paper.

2. Sprinkle the cubed chicken with the cayenne.

3. In a medium bowl, beat the eggs with ¼ cup of orange juice. Put the bread crumbs on a plate.

4. Dip the chicken into the egg mixture, then into the bread crumbs to coat. Place on the prepared baking sheet as you work.

5. Bake the chicken for 25 minutes, or until it registers 165°F on an instant-read thermometer. The juices will run clear and the chicken will be white inside.

6. Meanwhile, in a large saucepan, combine the remaining 1¾ cups of orange juice, the marmalade, soy sauce, cornstarch, ginger, and garlic powder and bring to a simmer over medium heat. Simmer the sauce for 8 to 10 minutes, stirring occasionally with a whisk, until thickened.

7. When the chicken is done, transfer to a serving bowl and pour the orange sauce over it.

Cooking tip: Raw rice triples in volume when it's cooked. To get 3 cups of rice, combine 1 cup raw white rice with 2 cups water or broth. Simmer, partially covered, for 15 to 20 minutes until tender. Brown rice takes twice as long to cook.

Green Chicken Enchiladas

Prep time: 15 minutes   **Cook time:** 50 minutes   **Serves 4**

Enchiladas are usually made with beef or pork, but this recipe combines chicken with green chiles and green salsa for a delicious twist on the classic recipe. Enchiladas are fussy to make, what with filling and rolling each tortilla, but here everything is combined into a casserole, so it's super quick.

Nonstick cooking spray

2 tablespoons olive oil

1 onion, chopped

3 garlic cloves, minced

1 jalapeño pepper, minced

4 cups shredded cooked chicken

1½ cups green salsa

1 (10-ounce) can green enchilada sauce

5 corn tortillas, cut into 1-inch-wide strips

1 cup sour cream

2 cups shredded pepper Jack cheese

1. Preheat the oven to 400°F. Coat a 9-by-13-inch baking dish with cooking spray and set aside.

2. In a large skillet, heat the olive oil over medium heat. Add the onion, garlic, and jalapeño and cook for 4 minutes, stirring occasionally, until tender.

3. Add the chicken, salsa, and enchilada sauce and simmer for 5 minutes.

4. To assemble the casserole, spread ½ cup of the chicken mixture in the prepared pan. Add half of the tortilla strips, half of the remaining chicken mixture, half of the sour cream, and half of the pepper Jack cheese on top. Repeat with the remaining tortilla strips, chicken, sour cream, and cheese.

5. Cover the pan with foil and bake for 30 minutes. Uncover and bake for 10 minutes longer, or until the casserole is bubbling and the cheese on top is melted and starting to brown. Serve.

Cooking tip: Most casseroles like this one can be made ahead of time. Assemble the casserole, cover with foil, and put in the refrigerator for up to 24 hours. When you are ready to eat, bake it, adding 5 to 10 minutes to the baking time.

Shrimp Pesto Pasta

Prep time: 15 minutes   **Cook time:** 15 minutes   **Serves 6**

Cooking pasta in just enough water so it absorbs all of it is a great way to start a one-pot meal; no draining is required. When the pasta is halfway cooked, you just add the rest of the ingredients and let everything simmer together until done. There's no faster way to get dinner on the table.

4 cups water

1 (16-ounce) package gemelli or ziti pasta

1 pound medium shrimp, peeled and deveined

2 cups frozen baby peas (no need to thaw)

1 (10-ounce) package basil pesto

½ cup heavy cream

½ cup grated Parmesan cheese

1. In a large saucepan, combine the water and pasta and bring to a boil over high heat. Reduce the heat to low and simmer for 6 minutes, stirring often.

2. Add the shrimp and simmer for 3 minutes longer.

3. Add the peas, pesto, and cream and simmer for 2 to 3 minutes longer, until the pasta is tender, the shrimp are firm, and the sauce has thickened slightly.

4. Stir in the Parmesan and serve.

Variation: You can use other liquid in place of the water in this recipe to add more flavor. Try using vegetable broth, chicken broth, or a combination of fish broth and water.

Baked Shrimp Risotto

Prep time: 15 minutes   **Cook time:** 35 minutes   **Serves 4**

Shrimp is a luxurious addition to risotto, which is already a luxurious dish. This simple recipe is a great idea for entertaining. Just add a green salad and some garlic bread and offer brownies for dessert.

2 tablespoons olive oil

1 onion, chopped

2 garlic cloves, minced

½ teaspoon sea salt

⅛ teaspoon freshly ground black pepper

1 cup Arborio rice

6 cups chicken broth

1 pound medium shrimp, peeled and deveined

½ cup grated Parmesan cheese

2 tablespoons butter

1. Preheat the oven to 400°F.

2. In a large, heavy ovenproof skillet with a tight-fitting lid, heat the olive oil over medium heat. Add the onion and garlic and cook, stirring occasionally, for 4 minutes.

3. Sprinkle with the salt and pepper, add the rice, and cook, stirring, for 2 minutes longer.

4. Add the broth and bring to a simmer. Cover the skillet with heavy-duty foil and top with the lid.

5. Transfer to the oven and bake for 20 minutes.

6. Remove the pan from the oven, remove the lid and foil, and stir. Add the shrimp but leave them on top of the rice. Cover the skillet with just the lid.

7. Return to the oven and bake for 8 to 10 minutes longer, until the shrimp are curled and pink.

8. Stir again and if the rice is tender but still slightly firm in the middle, it's done. If not, cover and bake for another 5 minutes. Then stir in the Parmesan and butter. Let stand for 3 minutes, then stir and serve.

Cooking tip: Rice doneness is determined by tasting. Taste a grain. You should be able to bite easily through the grain of rice, but there should be a bit of resistance in the center. The grain should not fall apart.

Crab and Lemon Linguine

Prep time: 15 minutes   **Cook time:** 15 minutes   **Serves 6**

Linguine is a long pasta, wider and thicker than spaghetti. The name means "little tongues" in Italian. It's the perfect consistency to pair with rich crabmeat and tart lemon sauce.

1 lemon

1 pound lump crabmeat

2 scallions, both green and white parts, thinly sliced

¼ teaspoon sea salt

⅛ teaspoon freshly ground black pepper

1 (16-ounce) package linguine

3 tablespoons butter, at room temperature

½ cup grated Parmesan cheese

1. Bring a large pot of water to a boil.

2. Meanwhile, grate 1 teaspoon lemon zest into a small bowl, then halve the lemon and squeeze in the juice.

3. Pick over the crabmeat, removing any cartilage. Add the crab to the lemon zest and lemon juice, along with the scallions, salt, and pepper and mix gently.

4. Add the linguine to the boiling water and cook for 8 to 9 minutes, until just al dente.

5. Drain the pasta, reserving ½ cup of the cooking water, and return it to the pot. Add the butter and mix until melted.

6. Add the crab mixture and enough reserved pasta water to make a sauce. Sprinkle with the Parmesan and serve.

Cooking tip: Pasta water is often used to create a sauce for pasta. The water contains starch from the pasta, so it can create a sauce with the other ingredients. It's a good idea to always reserve some pasta water before you drain it just in case your sauce needs it.

Spicy Tuna Burgers

Prep time: 15 minutes   **Cook time:** 15 minutes   **Serves 4**

Tuna burgers can be pretty bland and uninteresting. Not this recipe! Spicy crackers help form the burgers, which are also flavored with chipotle peppers. Serve these burgers with a fruit salad for a cooling contrast.

⅔ cup mayonnaise

3 chipotle peppers in adobo, minced

1 large egg, beaten

⅓ cup crushed spicy cheese crackers (about 20 crackers)

3 scallions, both green and white parts, finely chopped

1 (12-ounce) can white tuna, drained

2 tablespoons olive oil

4 onion buns, split and toasted

4 butter lettuce leaves

1 tomato, sliced

1. In a small bowl, combine the mayonnaise and chipotles.

2. In a medium bowl, combine the egg, crushed crackers, and scallions. Stir in half of the mayonnaise mixture, then add the tuna and mix. Form into 4 burgers.

3. In a large skillet, heat the olive oil over medium heat. Add the tuna burgers and cook for 3 to 5 minutes on each side, turning once, until the burgers are lightly browned.

4. Make sandwiches with the burgers, buns, the remaining mayonnaise mixture, lettuce, and tomato and serve.

Ingredient tip: There are two types of canned tuna: canned white and canned light. Canned white tuna is albacore, which is higher quality than light tuna, which is skipjack. Skipjack has a stronger, fishier flavor. Read labels carefully when you buy canned tuna.

Salmon with Cherry Glaze

Prep time: 15 minutes   **Cook time:** 10 minutes   **Serves 6**

Salmon is a healthy and versatile fish. Everyone should eat salmon a couple of times a week because it's loaded with omega-3 fatty acids, which help protect your heart and reduce inflammation. And it's delicious. This cherry glaze accents the nutty and mild flavor of salmon and makes the fish look beautiful, too.

1 (15-ounce) can dark cherries, drained

⅓ cup cherry preserves

2 tablespoons freshly squeezed lemon juice

6 skin-on salmon fillets (6 ounces each)

½ teaspoon sea salt

⅛ teaspoon freshly ground black pepper

1. In a medium bowl, mash the cherries with a potato masher or a large fork, leaving some bigger pieces. Stir in the cherry preserves and lemon juice and set aside.

2. Position an oven rack about 6 inches from the heat source and preheat the broiler to high.

3. Set the salmon fillets, skin-side down, on a broiler pan (or on a wire rack set on a rimmed baking sheet) and sprinkle with the salt and pepper.

4. Broil the salmon for 5 minutes, then remove from the oven and spoon some of the cherry mixture over the salmon.

5. Broil for another 3 to 5 minutes, until the salmon just flakes when tested with a fork.

6. Serve the salmon with the remaining cherry mixture on the side.

Ingredient tip: When fresh cherries are in season, you can use them in this recipe, but pitting the cherries will add another 20 minutes to the preparation time. To pit cherries, use a cherry pitter, or cut each cherry in half and pry out the pit.

Classic Pot Roast,
page 94

CHAPTER SEVEN
Beef and Pork Mains

Classic Pot Roast

Prep time: 15 minutes   **Cook time:** 4 hours   **Serves 6**

Pot roast is an American classic. Tender beef is cooked with carrots, onions, and potatoes in a one-pot meal that is comforting and satisfying. This recipe isn't difficult to make; it just takes some time in the oven. Searing the meat before it roasts adds flavor, but this step isn't necessary (see Cooking tip).

**1 chuck roast
(3 to 4 pounds)**

**1 teaspoon salt, plus
more to taste**

**1 teaspoon dried
marjoram leaves**

**¼ teaspoon freshly
ground black pepper**

**1 pound red
potatoes, quartered**

**1 pound carrots, cut
into chunks**

**2 onions, cut
into wedges**

2 cups beef stock

**3 tablespoons
all-purpose flour**

3 tablespoons butter

1. Preheat the oven to 350°F.

2. Sprinkle the roast with salt, marjoram, and pepper and rub into the meat. Put the meat into a Dutch oven. Surround with the potatoes, carrots, and onions. Pour the stock over.

3. Cover the Dutch oven, transfer to the oven, and roast for 3 to 4 hours, until the beef registers 200°F on an instant-read thermometer. At this temperature the collagen will have melted so the beef will be very tender.

4. Transfer the beef, which should be falling apart, to a platter and surround with the vegetables. Cover with foil to keep warm.

5. In a small bowl, combine the flour and butter and stir into the drippings remaining in the Dutch oven. Cook over medium-high heat for 2 minutes, stirring constantly with a whisk. Taste and add salt if necessary (salt is the secret to the best gravy) and cook until the flavor blooms and the gravy thickens, a few minutes longer. Serve with the beef and vegetables.

Ingredient tip: The cut used for pot roast is surprisingly inexpensive because the tougher cuts work best in this recipe. Boneless chuck roast has good marbling (fat content) and becomes very tender as it cooks for hours because the collagen in the meat breaks down into gelatin. More expensive cuts of meat aren't good for braising. Other cuts good for pot roast include brisket and round roast.

Cooking tip: If you want to take the time, sear the beef before it goes into the oven. Add 2 tablespoons olive oil to the Dutch oven and sear the beef on all sides; this should take about 15 minutes total. Then add the vegetables and proceed with the recipe.

Chipotle Tamale Pie

Prep time: 15 minutes   **Cook time:** 30 minutes   **Serves 6**

This tamale pie is simply a rich ground beef mixture that is topped with corn bread and baked. This classic recipe is easy to make, even if you don't use a corn muffin mix as most recipes do.

1½ pounds lean ground beef

1 (15-ounce) can black beans, drained and rinsed

1 (10-ounce) jar smooth taco sauce

1 cup frozen corn kernels

3 chipotle peppers in adobo, minced, plus 2 tablespoons adobo sauce

1 cup all-purpose flour

1 cup yellow cornmeal

1 teaspoon baking powder

¼ teaspoon sea salt

1 cup whole milk

¼ cup vegetable oil

1 large egg

1. Preheat the oven to 400°F.

2. In a 10-inch ovenproof skillet, cook the ground beef over medium heat for 6 to 8 minutes, stirring occasionally to break up the meat. Drain.

3. Add the black beans, taco sauce, corn, and minced chipotles to the beef and stir. Let simmer while you prepare the topping.

4. In a medium bowl, combine the flour, cornmeal, baking powder, and salt and stir. Make a well in the center and add the milk, oil, egg, and adobo sauce, stirring just until combined.

5. Spoon the cornmeal mixture over the beef in the skillet and spread evenly.

6. Transfer to the oven and bake for 25 to 35 minutes, until the topping is set and starting to brown. Serve.

Variation: You can add other ingredients to the beef mixture if you want. Add more chopped vegetables when you brown the beef, including chopped onions, minced garlic, red bell pepper, sliced mushrooms, or chopped zucchini.

Herbed Short Ribs with Slaw

Prep time: 15 minutes   **Cook time:** 3 hour 30 minutes   **Serves 4**

Beef short ribs are short ribs from the chuck section of the cow. They are similar to steaks but are too small to be sold as steaks, and they have a large bone. When cooked for a long period of time they become meltingly tender. In this recipe, they are served with a cool slaw for great contrast.

4 pounds bone-in beef short ribs

½ teaspoon sea salt

⅛ teaspoon freshly ground black pepper

2 tablespoons olive oil

1 onion, chopped

3 garlic cloves, minced

1 cup beef stock

1 bay leaf

1 (16-ounce) bag shredded red cabbage

1 Granny Smith apple, chopped

½ cup dried cranberries

½ cup ranch salad dressing

1. Preheat the oven to 350°F.

2. Sprinkle the ribs with salt and pepper. In a Dutch oven or large ovenproof skillet with a lid, heat the oil over medium heat. Add the ribs and brown on all sides, about 7 minutes. Transfer the ribs to a plate and set aside.

3. Add the onion and garlic to the drippings in the Dutch oven and cook for 4 minutes, or until tender.

4. Return the ribs to the Dutch oven and add the stock and bay leaf. Bring to a simmer.

5. Cover the Dutch oven or skillet and bake for 3 hours to 3 hours 30 minutes, or until the ribs are very tender.

6. While the ribs are baking, in a medium bowl, combine the cabbage, apple, cranberries, and salad dressing and toss. Cover and refrigerate.

7. When the ribs are done, discard the bay leaf. Serve the ribs with the slaw.

Ingredient tip: Bone-in short ribs have more flavor than boneless short ribs, which technically aren't short ribs at all, but rib meat separated from the bone. The bone-in ribs take longer to cook but are worth it.

Cooking tip: When browning beef and other meats, leave it alone until the meat easily releases from the pan. Don't pull on it and tear the meat. That's the best way to get an even sear.

Cheese-Stuffed Meatloaf

Prep time: 15 minutes   **Cook time:** 1 hour 10 minutes   **Serves 6**

Meatloaf is the ultimate comfort food. This recipe combines ground beef and pork sausage for more flavor. The melted cheese in the center of the meatloaf is so delicious. Serve this with some Classic Scalloped Potatoes (page 36) and a green salad.

1 onion, finely chopped

1 tablespoon butter

⅓ cup plain dried bread crumbs

1 large egg

2 tablespoons yellow mustard

½ teaspoon dried marjoram leaves

½ teaspoon sea salt

⅛ teaspoon freshly ground black pepper

1 pound lean ground beef

8 ounces pork sausage

1½ cups shredded Colby-Jack cheese

5 bacon slices

1. Preheat the oven to 375°F.

2. In a small skillet, combine the onion and butter and cook over medium heat for 3 to 4 minutes, until the onion is softened.

3. Transfer the onion to a large bowl and add the bread crumbs, egg, mustard, marjoram, salt, and pepper.

4. Add the beef and pork and mix gently but thoroughly with your hands.

5. Divide the meat in half. In a 9-by-13-inch baking dish, form half of the meat into a 9-by-5-inch rectangle on the bottom. Top with the cheese in a strip down the middle. Top with the remaining meat mixture and gently form into a loaf, pressing the sides so the cheese doesn't leak out during baking.

6. Drape the bacon over the meatloaf and tuck under the bottom.

7. Bake the meatloaf for 1 hour to 1 hour 10 minutes, until an instant-read thermometer registers 160°F. The meatloaf will feel firm and the juices will run clear. Make sure you don't get the thermometer probe into the cheesy center. Let stand for 10 minutes, then slice to serve.

Cooking tip: When making meatloaf, combine all the other ingredients first, then add the meat to keep the loaf tender. Also, meatloaf always slices better if it stands for 10 to 15 minutes after it finishes cooking.

One-Pot Spaghetti and Meatballs

Prep time: 15 minutes   **Cook time:** 15 minutes   **Serves 4**

The best way to save time when making spaghetti and meatballs is to cook everything in one pot, including the pasta and meatballs. And when the meatballs simmer in sauce rather than being browned in a pan, they are so tender. This classic recipe will become a mainstay in your kitchen.

1 (26-ounce) jar
  pasta sauce

2½ cups water

1 (8-ounce) can
  tomato sauce

1 teaspoon Italian
  seasoning

1 pound extra-lean
  ground beef

¼ cup Italian-style
  dried bread crumbs

1 large egg

1 (16-ounce)
  box spaghetti

½ cup grated
  Parmesan cheese

1. In a large skillet, combine the pasta sauce, water, tomato sauce, and Italian seasoning and bring to a simmer over medium heat.

2. Meanwhile, in a medium bowl, combine the beef, bread crumbs, and egg and mix gently but thoroughly. Put a sheet of parchment paper or foil on the counter. Pat the beef mixture into an 8-inch square on the paper. Cut into 25 squares.

3. Gently squeeze each square into a ball as you drop it into the simmering pasta sauce. Let the meatballs simmer for 3 minutes.

4. Add the pasta, making sure it's covered with the sauce. Simmer about 10 to 12 minutes longer, stirring occasionally, until the pasta is al dente and the meatballs are cooked through.

5. Sprinkle with the Parmesan and serve.

Cooking tip: Any type of tomato sauce simmering on the stove is likely to make a mess. Think about buying a splatter guard, which is a steel mesh round with a handle. Put that on top of the skillet to reduce splatter.

Salisbury Steak

Prep time: 15 minutes   **Cook time:** 1 hour 5 minutes   **Serves 6**

The title may say "steak," but Salisbury steak is simply a ground beef patty that is served in a mushroom sauce. This classic and old-fashioned recipe is easy to make. Serve with Creamy Mashed Potatoes (page 37) to soak up the wonderful sauce.

2 tablespoons butter

1 (8-ounce) package sliced mushrooms

1 onion, finely chopped

½ cup crushed cheese cracker crumbs

1 large egg

3 tablespoons ketchup

½ teaspoon sea salt

⅛ teaspoon freshly ground black pepper

1¾ pounds lean ground beef

2 cups beef stock

2 tablespoons cornstarch

2 tablespoons Worcestershire sauce

1. Preheat the oven to 350°F.

2. In a large skillet, melt the butter. Add the mushrooms and onion and cook for 10 minutes, stirring occasionally, until the mushrooms start to brown.

3. Meanwhile, in a large bowl, combine the cracker crumbs, egg, ketchup, salt, and pepper and mix well. Add the beef and mix gently but thoroughly. Form into 6 patties about ½ inch thick. Put the patties in a Dutch oven or ovenproof skillet with a lid.

4. To the mushrooms in the skillet, add the stock, cornstarch, and Worcestershire sauce and stir. Cook for 3 minutes or until thickened. Pour the sauce mixture over the patties in the Dutch oven.

5. Cover, transfer to the oven, and bake for 45 to 55 minutes, until the beef registers 160°F on an instant-read thermometer. The patties should be firm. Serve.

Ingredient tip: Ground beef is labeled regular, lean, and extra-lean, as well as named for the cut it is made from. This can be confusing; here's what you need to know. As a general guide, lean ground beef has about 22 percent fat, and extra-lean 10 to 15 percent fat. Ground chuck has the most fat at 20 percent; ground round has 15 to 20 percent fat, and ground sirloin 8 to 10 percent fat. When a ground beef recipe is made without browning and draining the beef, you must use a lean type, or the recipe will be greasy.

Hungarian Goulash

Prep time: 15 minutes   **Cook time:** 3 hours   **Serves 6**

Goulash is a classic Old World recipe that is essentially a thick beef stew. It is flavored with onions, caraway seeds, and paprika. It simmers for hours on the stovetop, filling your home with a wonderful fragrance while you relax.

2 tablespoons olive oil

1 onion, chopped

3 garlic cloves, minced

1½ pounds cubed chuck steak

1 tablespoon paprika

1 teaspoon caraway seeds

½ teaspoon sea salt

1½ pounds baby Yukon Gold potatoes

1 pound baby carrots

2 cups beef stock

1 (14.5-ounce) can diced tomatoes, undrained

2 tablespoons cornstarch

1. In a large skillet or Dutch oven, heat the olive oil over medium heat. Add the onion and garlic and cook for 2 minutes, or until crisp-tender.

2. Add the steak and cook for another 3 minutes, or until it starts to brown. Then sprinkle with the paprika, caraway seeds, and salt.

3. Add the potatoes, carrots, stock, and tomatoes and their juices and bring to a simmer. Reduce the heat to low, partially cover the pot, and simmer for 2 to 3 hours, until the beef is very tender.

4. Remove about ½ cup of liquid from the pan and combine in a small bowl with the cornstarch. Stir this mixture back into the goulash and simmer for 3 to 5 minutes to thicken the mixture. Serve.

Ingredient tip: Paprika is the classic spice for goulash. It comes in three types: plain or sweet, hot, or smoked. Any type is good in this recipe, depending on what flavors you enjoy.

Cooking tip: "Partially cover the pot" means that you put the lid on the pot but leave it slightly ajar so about an inch of the pot is open for steam to escape.

Spicy Orange Beef Stir-Fry

Prep time: 15 minutes   **Cook time:** 10 minutes   **Serves 4**

This fragrant and flavorful recipe is one of the best. Tender flank steak is quickly cooked with orange juice and veggies for a colorful and delicious meal. Serve over hot cooked rice to soak up the wonderful sauce.

½ cup orange juice

⅓ cup water

2 tablespoons
  reduced-sodium
  soy sauce

2 tablespoons
  cornstarch

⅛ teaspoon
  cayenne pepper

2 tablespoons
  peanut oil

1 pound flank steak,
  thinly sliced against
  the grain

1 onion, chopped

1 red bell pepper, sliced

1 jalapeño
  pepper, minced

1 cup frozen peas

1. In a small bowl, combine the orange juice, water, soy sauce, cornstarch, and cayenne and mix until combined. Set aside.

2. In a wok or large skillet, heat the peanut oil over medium heat. Add the steak and stir-fry for 2 minutes, or until the meat starts to brown. Transfer the meat to a plate.

3. Add the onion, bell pepper, and jalapeño to the wok and stir-fry for 3 to 4 minutes, until crisp-tender.

4. Return the steak to the wok and add the peas and stir-fry for 1 minute longer.

5. Stir the sauce and add to the wok. Stir-fry for 2 to 4 minutes to thicken the sauce.

Cooking tip: To slice flank steak "against the grain," look at the meat. You will see lines running through it; that's the "grain." Cut perpendicular to those lines so the steak will be tender when it's cooked.

Beef and Broccoli

Prep time: 15 minutes   **Cook time:** 10 minutes   **Serves 6**

This classic Chinese recipe is super-fast to make. It uses some ingredients you'll need to get in the international food aisle of the supermarket. For example, oyster sauce, which is rich and thick and tastes very meaty. It adds a real depth of flavor to this easy recipe. And bamboo shoots are tender and sweet, adding a nice floral note to the recipe.

1 cup beef stock

2 tablespoons oyster sauce

2 tablespoons reduced-sodium soy sauce

1 tablespoon honey

1 tablespoon cornstarch

1 pound top sirloin steak, thinly sliced

2 tablespoons peanut oil

3 cups broccoli florets

1 (8-ounce) can sliced bamboo shoots, drained

1 tablespoon sesame seeds

1. In a medium bowl, combine the beef stock, oyster sauce, soy sauce, honey, and cornstarch and mix well. Add the sliced steak and set aside.

2. In a wok or large skillet, heat the peanut oil over medium-high heat. Add the broccoli and stir-fry for 2 minutes, or until the broccoli is bright green. Transfer the broccoli to a plate.

3. Take the steak strips out of the marinade, add to the wok, and stir-fry for 2 minutes, or until the meat starts to brown.

4. Stir the marinade and add to the wok along with the broccoli and bamboo shoots. Stir-fry for 3 to 4 minutes to thicken the sauce.

5. Sprinkle with the sesame seeds and serve.

Ingredient tip: Other cuts of beef that are good for stir-fries include skirt steak, sirloin tip, and flank steak. Be sure to cut the beef against the grain for best results.

Pasta Bolognese

Prep time: 15 minutes   **Cook time:** 1 hour 15 minutes   **Serves 6**

Bolognese is a rich Italian meat sauce made with tomatoes, onion, beef, and herbs. It simmers for a long time, which thickens the sauce and enhances its flavors. Serve over linguine or fettuccine with garlic toast for a great meal.

1½ pounds ground beef (85/15)

1 onion, chopped

1 cup preshredded carrots

4 garlic cloves, minced

½ teaspoon sea salt

1 (28-ounce) can crushed tomatoes

1 cup red wine or beef stock

3 tablespoons tomato paste

1 bay leaf

1 teaspoon Italian seasoning

1 pound linguine or fettuccine

½ cup shredded Parmesan cheese

1. In a stockpot or Dutch oven, combine the beef, onion, carrots, and garlic. Sprinkle with the salt. Cook over medium heat for 7 to 9 minutes, stirring occasionally to break up the meat, until the meat is browned. Drain.

2. Add the crushed tomatoes, wine, tomato paste, bay leaf, and Italian seasoning and bring to a simmer. Simmer for 45 to 55 minutes, stirring occasionally, until the sauce has thickened. Discard the bay leaf.

3. Meanwhile, bring a large pot of water to a boil over high heat. Cook the pasta according to package directions until al dente.

4. Drain the pasta and serve the meat sauce over the pasta. Top with the Parmesan.

Ingredient tip: If you buy Parmesan cheese in a wheel instead of pre-grated, don't throw away the rind. Freeze it in pieces and use it in long simmering recipes like this one. The rind adds great flavor to tomato sauces. Discard the rind before serving.

Grilled Cheese, Peach, and Bacon Sandwiches

Prep time: 15 minutes   **Cook time:** 10 minutes   **Serves 6**

Grilled cheese sandwiches are super quick and easy to make. They can often be boring, but not this recipe. Bacon and peach preserves are added for great flavor and interest. This sandwich is baked in the oven, which means you don't have to stand over the stove flipping sandwiches.

¼ cup mayonnaise

6 tablespoons (¾ stick) butter, at room temperature

12 firm-textured white or whole wheat bread slices

1 cup shredded Havarti cheese

1 cup shredded provolone cheese

6 slices precooked bacon, heated as directed on the package and crumbled

1 peach, peeled and diced

½ cup peach jam

1. Preheat the oven to 425°F.

2. In a bowl, combine the mayonnaise and butter and spread it on one side of each bread slice. Place half of the bread, coated-side down, on a rimmed baking sheet. Set aside the remaining slices.

3. In a small bowl, combine the cheeses and toss. Divide the cheeses among the bread slices on the baking sheet. Top with the bacon and divide the diced peach and peach jam among the sandwiches.

4. Top with the remaining slices, coated-side up.

5. Bake the sandwiches for 5 minutes, then carefully turn with a spatula. Bake for another 4 to 6 minutes, until the sandwiches are golden brown. Serve.

Cooking tip: If not using precooked bacon, the best way to cook your own is in the oven. You don't need to turn it, and you also avoid all the splatter and mess. Line a rimmed baking sheet with foil. Put a rack in the pan and place the bacon on the rack (or use a broiler pan). Bake at 400°F for 12 to 16 minutes, until the bacon is crisp and browned.

Ravioli Lasagna

Prep time: 15 minutes   **Cook time:** 1 hour 15 minutes   **Serves 8**

This easy recipe uses frozen ravioli in place of the lasagna noodles to make assembly a breeze. Rich with sausage, ricotta, and lots of cheese, this delicious casserole can be made ahead of time, too, and baked when you need it.

Nonstick cooking spray

1 pound bulk sweet Italian sausage

1 onion, chopped

3 garlic cloves, minced

1 (26-ounce) jar spaghetti sauce

1 (14.5-ounce) can diced tomatoes, undrained

1 teaspoon Italian seasoning

1 (16-ounce) container part-skim ricotta cheese

1 cup shredded part-skim mozzarella cheese

1 cup shredded Parmesan cheese, divided

1 large egg

1 (25-ounce) package frozen cheese ravioli

1. Preheat the oven to 400°F. Coat a 9-by-13-inch baking dish with cooking spray and set aside.

2. In a large skillet, cook the sausage, onion, and garlic over medium heat for 4 to 6 minutes, stirring occasionally to break up the meat, until it is no longer pink. Drain.

3. Add the spaghetti sauce, diced tomatoes and their juices, and Italian seasoning and simmer for 5 minutes.

4. Meanwhile, in a medium bowl, combine the ricotta, mozzarella, ½ cup of Parmesan, and egg and mix well.

5. Spread one-third of the tomato sauce in the bottom of the prepared baking dish. Layer with half of the frozen ravioli and half of the ricotta mixture. Repeat the layers, adding one-third of the tomato sauce, the remaining half of the ravioli, remaining half of the ricotta, and the rest of the tomato sauce. Sprinkle with the remaining ½ cup of Parmesan.

6. Cover with foil and bake for 45 minutes. Uncover and bake for 15 to 20 minutes longer, until the lasagna is bubbling and the top is starting to brown. Let stand for 10 minutes, then cut into squares to serve.

Cooking tip: To make ahead of time, assemble the casserole and refrigerate. Bake in the next day or two, adding 10 minutes to the cooking time. You can also freeze the assembled casserole. Let thaw in the refrigerator overnight, then bake, adding 10 to 15 minutes to the cooking time.

Quick Hawaiian Pork Tacos

Prep time: 15 minutes   **Cook time:** 15 minutes   **Serves 4**

Bulk pork sausage is a very useful ingredient. It is a shortcut, combining ground pork with lots of seasonings for great flavor. About the Hawaiian moniker: Tacos made with SPAM or processed ham are a favorite on the islands. Pork sausage makes an admirable and more sophisticated substitute in these sweet and sour tacos.

1 pound bulk sweet Italian sausage

1 red onion, chopped

1 cup barbecue sauce

1 (8-ounce) can pineapple tidbits, drained

½ cup pineapple jam

1 jalapeño pepper, minced

4 to 6 (8- to 10-inch) flour tortillas

1 avocado, halved, peeled, and cubed

½ cup crumbled queso fresco cheese

1. In a large skillet, cook the sausage and red onion over medium heat for about 5 minutes, stirring occasionally to break up the meat, until it is cooked and browned. Drain.

2. Stir in the barbecue sauce and simmer for 5 minutes.

3. Meanwhile, in a small bowl, combine the pineapple tidbits, jam, and jalapeño.

4. To assemble the tacos, put some of the pork mixture on a tortilla. Top with the pineapple mixture, avocado, and queso fresco. Fold in half and eat.

Ingredient tip: If you can't find bulk Italian sausage, buy sausage links and remove the casings.

Ingredient tip: Queso fresco is a soft cheese similar to feta or goat cheese. It is fresh and slightly sour. If you can't find it, feta is a good substitute.

Roasted Garlic Pork Tenderloin

Prep time: 10 minutes   **Cook time:** 20 minutes   **Serves 6**

Pork tenderloin is the most wonderful cut. It has little fat and no waste but provides marvelous flavor. When roasted with garlic and herbs, it makes a delicious and super easy entrée. Be sure to buy plain pork tenderloin, because there are seasoned versions on the market.

2 pork tenderloins (1¼ pounds each)

½ teaspoon sea salt

⅛ teaspoon freshly ground black pepper

2 tablespoons butter

1 teaspoon dried thyme leaves

½ teaspoon dried basil

¼ teaspoon garlic powder

1. Preheat the oven to 425°F.
2. Set the pork tenderloins on a rimmed baking sheet and sprinkle with the salt and pepper.
3. In a small bowl, combine the butter, thyme, basil, and garlic powder. Spread this mixture over the pork.
4. Roast the pork for 18 to 23 minutes, or until the pork registers 145°F on an instant-read thermometer.
5. Remove the pan from the oven, cover the pork with foil, and let stand for 5 minutes, then slice to serve.

Cooking tip: When you are roasting foods at high temperatures you must make sure that your oven is clean, because any spilled food will smoke. Scrape off any food, then clean according to your oven's instruction manual.

Sweet and Sour Pork and Cabbage

Prep time: 15 minutes   **Cook time:** 30 minutes   **Serves 6**

Mild and tender pork adapts well to just about any flavor combination or cuisine. In this recipe pork is stir-fried with cabbage and a sweet and sour sauce. Most recipes like this use napa cabbage, but red cabbage is more flavorful and colorful.

½ cup chicken stock

¼ cup red wine vinegar

2 tablespoons reduced-sodium soy sauce

2 tablespoons light brown sugar

1 tablespoon cornstarch

3 tablespoons peanut oil, divided

1 pound pork tenderloin, cubed

4 cups preshredded red cabbage

1 red onion, chopped

⅓ cup dried cranberries

1. In a small bowl, combine the chicken stock, vinegar, soy sauce, brown sugar, and cornstarch. Set aside.

2. In a wok or large skillet, heat 2 tablespoons of peanut oil over medium-high heat. Add the pork and stir-fry for 3 to 5 minutes, until lightly browned. Remove the pork from the wok and set aside.

3. Add the remaining 1 tablespoon of peanut oil to the wok and add the cabbage and red onion. Stir-fry for 3 to 5 minutes, or until crisp-tender.

4. Return the pork to the wok. Stir the sauce and add it to the wok along with the dried cranberries. Stir-fry for 3 to 5 minutes, until the sauce is thickened, the pork registers 145°F on an instant-read thermometer, and the vegetables are tender. Serve.

Ingredient tip: Soy sauce isn't always gluten-free because it is usually made by combining soy and wheat. You can read labels to find a brand that states it is made without gluten, or you can substitute tamari, which is naturally gluten-free.

Peach Melba Icebox
Cake, page 112

CHAPTER EIGHT
Desserts, Condiments, and Staples

Peach Melba Icebox Cake 112

Creamy Brownies 113

Marzipan Cake with Strawberry Sauce 114

Orange-Mint Fruit Salad 115

Pecan Pie Bread Pudding 116

Chocolate Eton Mess 117

Lemon Rice Pudding 118

Spicy Honey Gingerbread 119

No-Roll Pie Crust 120

Pizza Dough 121

Homemade Grainy Honey Mustard 122

Garlic Vinegar 123

Easy Refrigerator Pickles 124

Barbecue Sauce 125

Pesto 126

Peach Melba Icebox Cake

Prep time: 15 minutes   **Chill time:** 12 hours   **Serves 12**

Peach Melba is an old-fashioned dessert made with peaches and raspberries. Those flavors are combined in a new way in this no-cook icebox dessert. It must be made ahead of time, giving the wafers time to soften in the whipped cream so that the cake holds together.

3 cups cold
  heavy cream

½ cup powdered sugar

1 teaspoon
  vanilla extract

½ cup peach jam
  or preserves

1 (11-ounce) box
  vanilla wafers

3 cups raspberries,
  plus more for garnish

Sliced peaches,
  for garnish

1. In a large bowl, with a hand mixer, combine the cream, sugar, and vanilla and beat on high for 5 to 6 minutes, until soft peaks form. Fold in the peach jam.

2. Spread about ¾ cup of whipped cream into a 9-inch springform pan. Top with some of the wafers in a single layer, not overlapping, and fill in the spaces with broken wafers. Then spread the wafers with about 1¾ cups of the cream to cover. Add a layer of the raspberries, pressing them into the cream. Repeat the layers two more times, trying to stagger the wafers so they aren't all in the same place in the pan.

3. Cover and chill for at least 12 hours or overnight.

4. To serve, run a knife around the edges of the pan and carefully remove the sides. Top with raspberries and sliced peaches, for garnish. Cut into wedges to serve. Store, covered, in the refrigerator up to 3 days.

Cooking tip: In order for heavy cream to whip well, it must be cold. In fact, for best results, chill the bowl and the beaters, too, for a couple of hours before you start the recipe.

Creamy Brownies

Prep time: 15 minutes   **Cook time:** 30 minutes   **Serves 8**

Brownies are the ultimate easy dessert. This recipe is creamy because it uses grated chocolate, which melts into the batter as the brownies bake. You can serve these unfrosted or make a simple chocolate frosting to top them.

Nonstick baking spray

1 cup (2 sticks) butter

1 cup granulated sugar

¾ cup packed light brown sugar

4 large eggs

1 tablespoon vanilla extract

1 cup all-purpose flour

½ cup unsweetened cocoa powder

⅛ teaspoon sea salt

1 cup milk chocolate chips

½ cup grated dark chocolate

1. Preheat the oven to 350°F. Coat a 9-by-13-inch baking pan with baking spray and set aside.

2. In a large saucepan, melt the butter over medium heat. Turn off the heat but leave the saucepan on the burner and add both sugars, beating thoroughly.

3. Remove the pan completely from the heat and beat in the eggs, one at a time, until combined. Stir in the vanilla. Add the flour, cocoa powder, and salt and mix. Add the chocolate chips and grated chocolate.

4. Spread the batter into the prepared pan and smooth into an even layer. Bake for 26 to 31 minutes, until a toothpick inserted near the center comes out with a few moist crumbs attached. Do not overbake.

5. Cool completely in the pan on a wire rack. Store covered at room temperature for up to 4 days.

Ingredient tip: To grate chocolate, use the fine side of a box grater.

Cooking tip: Brown sugar must always be measured by packing the sugar into the measuring cup or spoon. The sugar should hold its shape when you turn the cup over. And for best results, bake brownies and other desserts in a metal pan.

Marzipan Cake with Strawberry Sauce

Prep time: 15 minutes   **Cook time:** 30 minutes   **Serves 8**

Marzipan, or almond paste, is an ingredient used often in German cuisine. It adds a lovely nutty flavor and moist texture to this simple cake served with a fresh strawberry sauce. You can buy marzipan in the baking aisle of most grocery stores.

Nonstick baking spray

½ cup almond paste

⅓ cup butter, at room temperature

1 cup packed light brown sugar

2 large eggs

2 tablespoons orange juice

1 teaspoon vanilla extract

1⅓ cups all-purpose flour

1 teaspoon baking powder

½ teaspoon baking soda

⅛ teaspoon sea salt

2 cups whole strawberries

2 tablespoons powdered sugar

1 tablespoon freshly squeezed lemon juice

1. Preheat the oven to 350°F. Coat a 9-inch springform pan with baking spray and set aside.

2. In a large bowl, combine the almond paste and butter and beat until blended. Add the brown sugar and beat until combined. Beat in the eggs and orange juice until smooth. Beat in the vanilla.

3. Add the flour, baking powder, and baking soda, and salt and mix until smooth. Pour into the prepared pan.

4. Bake for 22 to 27 minutes, until the cake springs back in the center when lightly touched. Cool for 30 minutes in the pan on a wire rack, then remove the cake from the pan and cool completely.

5. To make the sauce, add the strawberries, powdered sugar, and lemon juice to a blender and blend under smooth. Serve with the cake. Store the cake, covered, at room temperature up to 4 days, and store the sauce in the refrigerator for up to 4 days.

Cooking tip: To remove a cake from a springform pan, run a knife carefully between the sides of the pan and the cake. Then remove the sides of the pan. Use a thin spatula to loosen the cake from the pan base, then transfer to a serving plate or cake stand.

Orange-Mint Fruit Salad

Prep time: 15 minutes   **Cook time:** 30 minutes   **Serves 4**

A fruit salad can be a wonderful dessert, especially in the summer when the best fruits are in season. In the winter, make this recipe with clementines, cubed apples, and pears. Combine the fruit with an orange-mint sauce for great flavor.

¼ cup orange juice

2 tablespoons minced
fresh mint leaves

2 tablespoons
powdered sugar

Pinch salt

4 cups fresh fruit
(cherries, raspberries,
strawberries,
blueberries, melon)

1. In a small bowl, combine the orange juice, mint, powdered sugar, and salt and mix well.

2. In a serving bowl, combine the fruits and drizzle with the orange-mint sauce. Serve.

Ingredient tip: The best way to tell if fruits are ripe is to feel them or smell them. Melons should give slightly when you press with your fingers. Cherries and strawberries should be firm but not hard and should smell sweet.

Pecan Pie Bread Pudding

Prep time: 15 minutes   **Cook time:** 50 minutes   **Serves 6**

Bread pudding is an old-fashioned dessert that gets a twist—and some texture—by adding pecans coated in a brown sugar syrup. Serve it warm from the oven with some cold vanilla ice cream on the side.

Nonstick baking spray

½ cup (1 stick) butter

⅓ cup light corn syrup

1 cup packed light brown sugar, divided

2 cups small pecan halves

2 cups whole milk

4 large eggs

½ cup granulated sugar

1 tablespoon vanilla extract

1 (16-ounce) loaf French bread, cubed

1. Preheat the oven to 375°F. Coat a 9-by-13-inch baking pan with baking spray and set aside.

2. In a medium saucepan, melt the butter with the corn syrup. Add ½ cup of brown sugar and bring to a simmer. Simmer the mixture about 3 minutes, until it combines and forms a sauce. Stir in the pecans and remove from the heat.

3. In a large bowl, combine the remaining ½ cup of brown sugar, the milk, eggs, granulated sugar, and vanilla and beat until combined.

4. Spread half of the bread in the prepared pan and, using a slotted spoon, remove some of the pecans from the syrup and sprinkle over the bread. Repeat the layering once.

5. Pour the egg mixture over the bread mixture and let stand for 10 minutes, pushing the bread down into the liquid from time to time.

6. Drizzle the syrup from the pecans over all.

7. Bake for 40 to 50 minutes, until the mixture is set and browning on top. Let cool for 30 minutes, then serve.

Ingredient tip: This recipe works best with bread that is slightly stale. So, buy a loaf of bread and set it on the counter for a couple of days. You can also cube the bread the day before you want to make this dessert and leave it uncovered overnight.

Chocolate Eton Mess

Prep time: 15 minutes   **Serves 6**

Eton Mess is a classic British dessert that is a combination of whipped cream, meringue, and berries. It can be eaten immediately, so the meringues are still crisp, or chilled before serving, so the meringues absorb moisture from the cream and become soft and creamy. This chocolate version is delicious.

1½ cups heavy cream

⅓ cup powdered sugar

¼ cup unsweetened cocoa powder

2 teaspoons vanilla extract

1 (4-ounce) package mini meringue cookies

2 cups raspberries

1. In a large bowl, with a hand mixer, combine the cream, powdered sugar, cocoa powder, and vanilla and beat on high for about 4 minutes, or until stiff peaks form.

2. Crumble the meringue cookies, leaving some larger pieces, and fold into the cream.

3. In six parfait glasses, layer the meringue mixture with the raspberries.

4. Serve immediately or cover and chill for a few hours before serving.

Variation: If you can't find mini meringue cookies, you can use 4 or 5 large meringue nests, which are used to make individual desserts. Just crumble them up.

Lemon Rice Pudding

Prep time: 15 minutes   **Cook time:** 2 hours   **Serves 6**

Rice pudding is the ultimate old-fashioned dessert. And it's very inexpensive, which is probably why it has been so popular through the decades. Lemon is the perfect partner for the tender rice and creamy sauce.

2 tablespoons butter, at room temperature

3½ cups whole milk

½ cup long-grain white rice

1 cup heavy cream

½ cup sugar

1 tablespoon finely grated lemon zest

⅓ cup freshly squeezed lemon juice

1 teaspoon vanilla extract

1. Preheat the oven to 325°F. Grease a 9-inch square baking pan with the butter.

2. In the pan, combine the milk, rice, cream, sugar, lemon zest, lemon juice, and vanilla, and stir gently. Put the dish on a baking sheet to protect against spillovers.

3. Bake, stirring thoroughly, but gently, three times during the first hour, for 2 hours to 2 hours 30 minutes, until the rice is tender and the liquid has been mostly absorbed.

4. Cool on a wire rack for at least 30 minutes before serving.

Cooking tip: The best way to zest a lemon is to use a fine grater or a rasp. Always zest the lemon before you cut it to squeeze the juice. And to get the most juice out of a lemon, firmly roll it on the countertop before you cut it to break up the cells in the flesh.

Spicy Honey Gingerbread

Prep time: 15 minutes   **Cook time:** 35 minutes   **Serves 12**

Gingerbread is a classic recipe that was hugely popular in the 1950s. This version uses honey instead of molasses, which can be bitter, and lots of spices. Serve it warm with a scoop of butter pecan ice cream.

Nonstick baking spray

1 cup packed light brown sugar

½ cup (1 stick) butter, at room temperature

¾ cup honey

3 large eggs

1 cup whole milk

3 cups all-purpose flour

1 tablespoon ground ginger

2 teaspoons grated peeled fresh ginger

1 teaspoon ground cinnamon

¼ teaspoon ground nutmeg

Pinch sea salt

1. Preheat the oven to 350°F. Coat a 9-by-13-inch baking pan with baking spray and set aside.

2. In a large bowl, using a large spoon, beat the brown sugar and butter until creamy. Beat in the honey. Add the eggs, one at a time, beating well after each addition. Stir in the milk.

3. Add the flour, ground ginger, fresh ginger, cinnamon, nutmeg, and salt and mix until combined.

4. Pour the batter into the prepared pan.

5. Bake for 35 to 40 minutes, until a toothpick inserted into the center comes out clean.

6. Cool on a wire rack for at least 30 minutes before cutting into squares to serve.

Ingredient tip: To peel the ginger, use a spoon to pull the skin off. Then grate the ginger on the fine side of a box grater or with a rasp-style grater.

No-Roll Pie Crust

Prep time: 15 minutes   **Cook time:** 12 minutes   **Makes 2 pie crusts**

You don't have to have a rolling pin to make a pie crust. With this easy recipe you just pat the dough into the pan. This recipe can be used for quiches, dessert pies, and freeform pies.

2½ cups all-purpose flour

½ teaspoon sea salt

¾ cup vegetable oil

2 tablespoons butter, melted

¼ cup cold water

1. In a large bowl, combine the flour and salt and mix well. Add the oil and melted butter and 2 tablespoons of water. Stir well until a dough forms. You may need to add more water, depending on how dry the dough is. You want a dough that is firm but not dry.

2. Divide the dough in half; each half will make one single crust pie.

3. When ready to make a crust, break the dough in pieces and press into the bottom and up the sides of a 9-inch pie pan. Crimp the edges by pinching them between your thumb and forefinger.

4. **For a filled pie:** Add the filling and bake the pie according to the recipe directions.

5. **For a baked pie shell:** Prick the bottom and sides of the crust with a fork. Bake at 375°F for 10 to 14 minutes, until the pie shell is light golden brown. Cool on a wire rack before filling.

Cooking tip: You can freeze pie dough. Just form the dough into a disc, wrap well in plastic wrap, and put into a freezer bag. Label the bag with the date. To use, let the dough thaw overnight in the refrigerator and use as directed. The dough will keep in the freezer for 6 months.

Pizza Dough

Prep time: 15 minutes   **Cook time:** 15 minutes   **Serves 6**

Pizza dough is easy to make. And it's fun, too. This easy recipe uses yeast and takes some time to rise, but it's so much better than those doughs in a tube. Make this on the weekend or make the dough and let it rise in the refrigerator overnight for fast pizza the next day.

2 cups all-purpose flour, plus more for dusting

½ cup yellow cornmeal, plus 2 tablespoons

2 (¼-ounce) packets active dry yeast

½ teaspoon salt

½ cup warm water (120°F)

¼ cup whole milk

2 tablespoons olive oil, plus more for greasing

1. In a large bowl, combine the flour, ½ cup of cornmeal, the yeast, and salt and mix well.

2. Add the warm water (see tip), milk, and olive oil to the flour and mix until a dough forms. You may need to add more water or flour to get a dough that is firm but malleable.

3. Knead the dough on a floured surface for a few minutes. Then put the dough into a greased bowl, turn it so it is greased all over, and cover the bowl. Let rise for 2 hours at room temperature, or 24 hours in the refrigerator.

4. When you're ready to make pizza, preheat the oven according to whatever pizza recipe you are using. Divide the dough in half. Grease 2 baking sheets and sprinkle each with 1 tablespoon of remaining cornmeal. Roll the dough out onto each sheet as directed in the recipe. Let the dough rest while you prepare the toppings you want to use.

5. Top the crusts and bake according to your recipe.

6. You can freeze the dough or a partially baked crust. Wrap the dough in parchment paper and put into a freezer bag. Freeze for up to 3 months. To use, let thaw overnight in the refrigerator. Alternatively, partially bake the rolled-out crust on a baking sheet by baking at 400°F for 8 minutes, then cool, wrap, and freeze.

Cooking tip: The water for the dough should be about 120°F, which is the average temperature from a hot water tap. Or you can microwave the water until it feels very warm when you touch it.

Cooking tip: To knead dough, put it on a floured surface. Fold the dough over on itself and push it away from you with the heel of your hand. Give the dough a one-quarter turn and repeat until the dough feels smooth and springy.

Homemade Grainy Honey Mustard

Prep time: 15 minutes   **Makes 1½ cups**

Homemade mustard is simple to make and really delicious. This recipe is quite strong. If you want a milder mustard, let it sit in the refrigerator for a few weeks, stirring every day to release some of the aromatic sulfur compounds.

⅔ cup apple
   cider vinegar

½ cup yellow
   mustard seeds, plus
   2 tablespoons

⅓ cup water

2 tablespoons honey

1 tablespoon
   mustard powder

½ teaspoon sea salt

1. In a clean screw-top glass jar, combine the vinegar, ½ cup of mustard seeds, water, honey, mustard powder, and salt. Let stand for 24 hours.

2. Transfer three-quarters of the mustard mixture to a blender and blend until almost smooth.

3. Return the blended mustard mixture to the jar and add the remaining 2 tablespoons of mustard seeds.

4. Cover and refrigerate for 3 to 5 days, stirring every day, until you like the flavor. Store in an airtight container in the refrigerator for up to 3 months.

Variation: You can also use brown mustard seeds in this recipe for a stronger mustard flavor or use a combination of the two. Or omit the honey for plain mustard. Or use ⅓ cup white wine instead of the water for a variation on Dijon mustard.

Garlic Vinegar

Prep time: 15 minutes   **Makes 2 cups**

Flavored vinegar is delicious to use in salad dressings, or to add some zip to vegetable casseroles. And it is so easy to make. You can put just about anything into vinegar, from garlic to chives to raspberries.

8 garlic cloves

**2 cups white
   wine vinegar**

1. Smash the garlic with the side of a chef's knife and peel it.
2. In a clean screw-top glass jar, combine the vinegar and garlic. Seal the jar and let stand for 1 week before using.
3. You can replenish the vinegar as you use it. It will keep for 6 months; after that time, strain the vinegar and return to the jar. Add fresh garlic.

Ingredient tip: Look for unusual types of garlic to use in this recipe. The different kinds include softneck and hardneck; within those two types, you can often find garlic that is colored. Look for red garlic, purple stripe, or Creole garlic, which is pink. You can also add chives, rosemary and other fresh herbs, tiny chiles, or grated fresh ginger for other types of flavored vinegar.

Easy Refrigerator Pickles

Prep time: 15 minutes   **Makes 2 pints**

Homemade pickles are impressive to offer to guests. And they are so simple to make. Look for English cucumbers for this recipe; they have a very small seed area and are sold unwaxed. You can make these pickles as mild or as spicy as you like. Serve them on their own, with burgers, or add them to potato salad or pasta salads.

2 English cucumbers (12 inches long)

4 dill sprigs

1 cup distilled white vinegar

⅔ cup water

¼ cup sugar

1½ teaspoons kosher salt

1 teaspoon mustard seeds

½ teaspoon celery seed

Pinch red pepper flakes (optional)

1. Rinse the cucumber and slice into ¼-inch-thick rounds. Place in a large heatproof bowl with the dill.

2. In a small saucepan, combine the vinegar, water, sugar, salt, mustard seeds, and celery seed. Bring to a simmer and simmer for 1 to 2 minutes, until the sugar is dissolved.

3. Slowly pour the vinegar mixture over the cucumber slices in the bowl. Add the pepper flakes (if using). Cover and store in the refrigerator for a few days before using.

4. After the pickles cool you can transfer them and the liquid into clean pint jars. Make sure you leave ½-inch headspace in the jar. Store in the refrigerator for up to 3 weeks.

Cooking tip: Because this recipe isn't heat-processed like other canned recipes are, you must not reduce the amount of vinegar. If you use apple cider vinegar, make sure it is 5 percent acidity for food safety reasons.

Barbecue Sauce

Prep time: 10 minutes   **Cook time:** 20 minutes   **Makes 3 cups**

Your own homemade barbecue sauce is delicious for all kinds of grilling. Brush it onto hamburgers about 5 minutes before they are done, or brush onto chicken. It's also delicious served as a dip for French fries.

1 tablespoon olive oil

1 onion, chopped

1 (8-ounce) can tomato sauce

1 cup ketchup

½ cup apple cider vinegar

½ cup packed light brown sugar

3 tablespoons Dijon mustard

2 tablespoons freshly squeezed lemon juice

⅛ teaspoon red pepper flakes

1. In a large saucepan, heat the olive oil over medium heat. Add the onion and cook for 3 minutes, stirring occasionally, until crisp-tender.

2. Add the tomato sauce, ketchup, vinegar, brown sugar, mustard, lemon juice, and pepper flakes and simmer for 15 to 17 minutes, stirring occasionally, to blend the flavors.

3. Cool, then transfer to an airtight container and store in the refrigerator for up to 5 days.

Variation: This easy recipe is quite versatile. Add more mustard for a spicier taste. Or add more red pepper flakes or a minced jalapeño or two for a hotter sauce.

Pesto

Prep time: 15 minutes   **Makes 1½ cups**

Pesto is an uncooked Italian sauce made mostly of basil leaves, olive oil, and Parmesan cheese. This recipe uses baby spinach, too, to cut down on the cost and to add a fresh, slightly bitter note. Use this recipe as a salad dressing by adding some mayonnaise to the pesto. Or beat it into some cream cheese to use a dip. Add the pesto to hot cooked pasta along with some pasta cooking water for a pasta sauce or brush it onto grilled meats for a flavorful finish.

⅓ cup olive oil

1 cup packed fresh basil leaves

½ cup packed baby spinach

½ cup chopped walnuts or pine nuts

½ cup grated Parmesan cheese

3 garlic cloves, peeled and halved

½ teaspoon sea salt

3 tablespoons water

1. In a blender, combine the olive oil, basil, spinach, walnuts, Parmesan, garlic, and salt and process until the basil and spinach are finely chopped. You will need to stop the blender and stir the mixture and scrape down the sides a few times.

2. While the blender is running, gradually add enough water, a tablespoon at a time, to form a sauce.

3. Transfer to a sealed container and store in the refrigerator for up to 3 days.

Cooking tip: You can freeze this pesto for longer storage. Put into ice cube trays and freeze until solid. Then keep in a resealable plastic freezer bag. Each cube of pesto is about 2 tablespoons.

Variation: For a chunkier pesto, add some more hand chopped nuts after the pesto is finished.

Recipe Notes

Recipe Notes

Recipe Notes

Recipe Notes

_____
_____
_____
_____
_____
_____
_____
_____
_____
_____
_____
_____
_____
_____
_____
_____
_____

Measurement Conversions

Volume Equivalents	U.S. Standard	U.S. Standard (ounces)	Metric (approximate)
Liquid	2 tablespoons	1 fl. oz.	30 mL
	¼ cup	2 fl. oz.	60 mL
	½ cup	4 fl. oz.	120 mL
	1 cup	8 fl. oz.	240 mL
	1½ cups	12 fl. oz.	355 mL
	2 cups or 1 pint	16 fl. oz.	475 mL
	4 cups or 1 quart	32 fl. oz.	1 L
	1 gallon	128 fl. oz.	4 L
Dry	⅛ teaspoon	–	0.5 mL
	¼ teaspoon	–	1 mL
	½ teaspoon	–	2 mL
	¾ teaspoon	–	4 mL
	1 teaspoon	–	5 mL
	1 tablespoon	–	15 mL
	¼ cup	–	59 mL
	⅓ cup	–	79 mL
	½ cup	–	118 mL
	⅔ cup	–	156 mL
	¾ cup	–	177 mL
	1 cup	–	235 mL
	2 cups or 1 pint	–	475 mL
	3 cups	–	700 mL
	4 cups or 1 quart	–	1 L
	½ gallon	–	2 L
	1 gallon	–	4 L

Oven Temperatures

Fahrenheit	Celsius (approximate)
250°F	120°C
300°F	150°C
325°F	165°C
350°F	180°C
375°F	190°C
400°F	200°C
425°F	220°C
450°F	230°C

Weight Equivalents

U.S. Standard	Metric (approximate)
½ ounce	15 g
1 ounce	30 g
2 ounces	60 g
4 ounces	115 g
8 ounces	225 g
12 ounces	340 g
16 ounces or 1 pound	455 g

Glossary

al dente: Italian for "to the bite," food that is cooked to be firm; pasta is frequently cooked this way

beat: Mixing or stirring ingredients rapidly in a circular motion to make a smooth mixture, using a whisk, spoon, or mixer

bake: To cook foods that don't have a solid structure (like bread or cakes) with dry heat in an oven

brown: To cook over high heat, usually on top of the stove, to brown food

bubbling: When a pot of sauce or water comes to a boil, and you see bubbles at the surface

chill: To chill food in a refrigerator until it is thoroughly cooled but not frozen

core: To remove the seeds or tough woody centers from fruits and vegetables

combine: To mix two or more food ingredients to create a mixture

drippings: Fat and juices drawn from meat during cooking

drizzle: To pour liquid, like an oil or dressing, back and forth over food in a fine stream

garnish: Something added to the top of a finished dish for visual appeal

grate: To reduce food to small shreds

mince: To cut food into very small pieces, usually so it can be dissolved when cooking; garlic, herbs and other aromatics are often minced

packed: When the measuring cup or spoon is filled to the top, the ingredient is pushed down, and then a bit more is added to top it off; often done with brown sugar and chopped fresh herbs

roast: To cook food with a solid structure (like vegetables or meats) with dry heat from an oven

sauté: To cook food in a pan over relatively high heat with a small amount of fat; similar to panfrying, except the heat is a bit higher because the pieces of food are smaller and cook faster

sear: To cook food at intense heat so that a crust is formed; seals in the flavor and the juices of meats, poultry, and seafood

shred: To tear into long, narrow pieces

simmer: To cook slowly over low heat just below the boiling point; you will start to see small bubbles

softened: When foods like butter and cream cheese are taken out of the refrigerator and brought to room temperature

"to taste": As much or little of an ingredient as you would like

whisk: To beat or stir with a light, rapid movement; also a kitchen tool that does this

zest: The outer, colored part of the peel of citrus fruit

Index

About the Author

Linda Larsen is an author and home economist who has been developing recipes for years. She was the Busy Cook's Guide at About.com for 15 years, writing about how to cook, food safety, and quick cooking. She has written 46 cookbooks since 2005, including *The Complete Air Fryer Cookbook* and *The Complete Slow Cooking for Two Cookbook*, as well as *Eating Clean for Dummies*. Linda has worked for the Pillsbury Company since 1988, creating and testing recipes and working for the Pillsbury Bake-Off. She holds a Bachelor of Arts in biology from St. Olaf College, and a Bachelor of Science with high distinction in food science and nutrition from the University of Minnesota.

CPSIA information can be obtained
at www.ICGtesting.com
Printed in the USA
JSHW041124151120
9511JS00003B/5